THE BEST
TEEN
WRITING
OF 2008

D0370829

For information or permission contact:
Alliance for Young Artists & Writers, Inc.
557 Broadway
New York, NY 10012
212-343-6493
www.artandwriting.org

Anthology printing, September 2008
ISBN-13: 978-0-545-13390-9
ISBN-10: 0-545-13360-2

THE ALLIANCE FOR YOUNG ARTISTS & WRITERS PRESENTS

THE BEST
TEEN

FOREWORD BY
CHUCK PALAHNIUK
EDITED BY
TEMNETE SEBHATU

WRITING
OF 2008

SELECTED
NATIONAL
AWARD
WINNERS
FROM THE
SCHOLASTIC
ART & WRITING
AWARDS

ABOUT THE BEST TEEN WRITING OF 2008

The works featured in *The Best Teen Writing of 2008* are selected from The Scholastic Art & Writing Awards, a national program presented by the Alliance for Young Artists & Writers, which recognizes talented teenagers in the visual and literary arts. The Awards were founded in 1923 to celebrate the accomplishments of creative students and extend to them the same opportunities for recognition as their athletic and academic classmates.

This year, more than 100,000 artworks and manuscripts were submitted to 76 regional affiliates. Professional artists, authors, educators and creative industry leaders reviewed the works, without knowledge of the students' identities and with no restriction on the content, looking for excellence in three criteria: technical skill, originality, and the emergence of a personal voice.

Approximately 30,000 students were recognized on the local level. Of those students, 1,139 received national awards. These young artists and writers have joined the ranks of artists and authors such as Richard Avedon, Truman Capote, Bernard Malamud, Carolyn Forché, Philip Pearlstein, Sylvia Plath, Joyce Carol Oates, Joyce Maynard, Andy Warhol and countless others who won awards when they were teenagers.

This year, 389 young writers received national recognition through The Awards. Forty-one were chosen for *The Best Teen Writing of 2008*. The writing selected represents the diversity of the national award winners, including age and grade, gender, genre, geography and subject matter. A complete listing of national award winners and a broader selection of works from The Awards can be found on our Web site at www.artandwriting.org.

To learn how to submit writing to The Scholastic Art & Writing Awards of 2009, visit www.artandwriting.org.

CONTENTS

EDITOR'S INTRODUCTION 10
—Temnete Sebhatu

A MESSAGE FROM THE NATIONAL COUNCIL OF TEACHERS
OF ENGLISH 12
—Kent Williamson

SNAKES AND SPIDERS 14
—Chuck Palahniuk

PORTFOLIO GOLD AWARDS

Graduating high school seniors may submit a portfolio of 3-8 works
for review by authors, educators, and literary professionals.
Winners of the General Writing Portfolio and Non-fiction Portfolio
Gold Award receive $10,000 scholarships.

HOMETOWN HARMONICS, *Short Story* 18
SUNDAYS ARE FOR LOVERS, *Short Story* 21
TO LILY SPELLMAN, *Short Short Story* 25
—Emma Morrison, Brooklyn, NY

DATE OF RELEASE, *Short Story* 27
NAMES, *Short Story* 37
SPAM MAIL, *Short Story* 42
—Jasmine Hu, San Jose, CA

THE NUMB ACRE, *Poetry* 51
HAS PASSED, *Poetry* 52
MY FAVORITE PLACES FOR YOUR HANDS, *Poetry* 54
—Virginia Pfaehler, North Charleston, SC

NOISE, *Poetry* 55
ORANGES, *Short Story* 57
SWEAT, *Personal Essay/Memoir* 65
—Vivian Truong, New York, NY

STARGAZING, *Personal Essay/Memoir* 69
THE LEFT AND THE LEAVING, *Personal Essay/Memoir* 77
—Victoria Cole, Greenville, SC

SELECTIONS FROM THE GOLD & SILVER AWARDS

Students in grades 7–12 submit work in eleven writing categories. This year, more than 20,000 writing submissions were reviewed by authors, educators, and literary professionals. Gold and Silver Awards were bestowed on works that demonstrated originality, technical skill and emergence of a personal voice.

TOURIST, *Personal Essay/Memoir* 88
—Amelia Wolf, Portland, OR

THE CHURCH OF GOD WITH SIGNS FOR FOLLOWERS
    WITHOUT DWELLINGS, *Poetry* 92
—Wynne Hungerford, Greenville, SC

THE DREAMBOOK FOR INCONSEQUENTIAL LIVES, *Short Short Story* . . 94
—Alice Rhee, Demarest, NJ

EL QUATRO DE JULIO, *Personal Essay/Memoir* 97
—MacKenzie Jacoby, Provo, UT

AS THIN OF SUBSTANCE AS THE AIR?, *Personal Essay/Memoir* 103
—Matthew Llarena, Miami Beach, FL

BENEATH THE SNOW: A MEMOIR, *Personal Essay/Memoir* 113
—Eric Kofman, Cary, NC

THE TRANSFORMATION, *Short Story* 119
—Elizabeth Cozart, Cedar Falls, IA

SLIP ROAD, *Personal Essay/Memoir* 122
—Cleo O'Brien-Udry, New Haven, CT

STEPS TO WORLD DOMINATION, *Humor* 126
—Paul Melcher, Houston, TX

THE TEA EGG, *Short Short Story* 129
—Xinhe Shen, Danville, CA

HELMETS AND SUPPOSED OXYGEN, *Poetry* 132
—Sean Kaellner, Indianapolis, IN

THAT SPECIAL TIME OF YEAR, *Personal Essay/Memoir* 134
—Gabe Lewin, Pennington, NJ

TIME IN TERMS OF NATURE, *Poetry* 138
—Maxine McGredy, New York, NY

BIRTHRIGHT, *Short Story* 140
—Alen Butt, Greenville, SC

SESAME STREET WHEN THE CAMERA'S OFF, *Dramatic Script* 149
—Aidan Graham, Brooklyn, NY

PH.D., *Poetry* 158
—Sara Carnick, Greenville, SC

CARAMEL, *Short Story* 160
—Matthew Joseph Disler, Richmond, VA

SHEOL, *Science Fiction/Fantasy* 166
—Paula Albaneze, Honolulu, HI

A, B, C, D, S, E, X, *Personal Essay/Memoir* 171
—Katie Eisenberg, Greenwich, CT

CIVIL SUCKSTON, *Poetry* 174
—Steven Niedbala, Waynesburg, PA

HERE'S AN INCONVENIENT TRUTH: NO ONE CARES, *Journalism* ... 176
—Erika Turner, Henderson, NV

THE TWO-MINUTE JOURNEY HOME WAS NOT, HOWEVER,
   WITHOUT ITS PROBLEMS, *Personal Essay/Memoir* 180
—Mark Warren, New York, NY

DEAD TREES, *Personal Essay/Memoir* 184
—Charlie Green, North Hollywood, CA

CURRENT, *Short Story* 187
—Kevin Hong, Natick, MA

ON AMERICAN IDENTITY, *Journalism* 197
—Dina Abdulhadi, Alpharetta, GA

TO WAIT IN ROME, *Short Story* 199
—Avital Chizhik, Elizabeth, NJ

DARE, *Short Short Story* 205
—Grace McNamee, Washington, D.C.

I DON'T WANT TO SLAM, *Poetry* 209
—Haydil Henriquez, Bronx, NY

THE SIZE OF A SMALL COFFIN, *Short Story* 212
—Becky McCarthy, Greens Farms, CT

LETTER TO READERS OF COSMO GIRL—"SKIN AND BONES"
Journalism 216
—Danniah Daher, Edgewood, KY

DEAF AND—SMART? *Personal Essay/Memoir* 219
—Rachel Kolb, Albuquerque, NM

REGRET #17 FROM ABIGAIL'S DIARY, *Poetry* 226
—Allison Cummings, Shelby, NC

HATS, *Poetry* 228
—Daniel Ross, New York, NY

THE GENERAL STORE, *Short Story* 229
—Jessi Glueck, Leawood, KS

OSTRICHES, *Short Story* 237
—Sharon Jan, Santa Ana, CA

JINGLE BEARS AND RAW SQUID, *Humor* 246
—Yumi Shiroma, Dobbs Ferry, NY

SPECIAL THANKS 252
ABOUT THE AUTHORS 253
NATIONAL WRITING JURORS 261
REGIONAL AFFILIATES 262
PARTNERSHIP OPPORTUNITIES 266
ABOUT THE ALLIANCE FOR YOUNG ARTISTS & WRITERS 267
ALLIANCE BOARD AND STAFF 269
HOW TO APPLY: OPPORTUNITIES FOR CREATIVE TEENS 271
HOW TO DONATE 272

EDITOR'S INTRODUCTION

"Writing is not a spectator sport." That is an aphorism—"a pithy observation that contains a general truth"—that was endlessly recited to me throughout high school. I'm still not entirely sure what it means. My best guess is it's a restatement of the obvious: certain events mandate a captive audience—calf-roping, roller derbies, controlled explosions—and others do not. While the final result is always thrilling, the writing process is not a sight that would inspire most to purchase popcorn or wear a beer hat. I have been known to stare, entranced, at footage of paramecium dividing, but I would not have paid for front-row seats for "Ernest Hemingway Idles at His Typewriter." Maybe others would gladly look on as Raymond Carver forlornly stubbed out a cigarette, but it's hardly enough to make me want to hoist a gigantic foam finger in the air.

If writing is a sport, what are the rules? Are there teams? I like the idea of approaching my desk in a mesh jersey or elbow pads. A large, distant loudspeaker would blare the first bars of a popular rock song as I open my laptop. Commentators would appreciatively note my keystrokes and posture. I might be wearing tube socks.

In keeping with this metaphor, let's say that we, aspiring writers, are a team. We howl fearsomely and stomp in the locker room before the game. We trot onto the field. The stadium lights are directly above; you imagine that you are a car in a showroom, only limber and intimidating. The opposition emerges faintly, like a mirage. They heckle you as they move closer. The usual topics are cited: your intelligence, appearance, and various unmentionables involving your mother. Your resolve begins to crumble. You wonder why their voices sound familiar until you realize the figure approaching from the end of the field is actually you. Slowly, you retreat to the sidelines.

Such is the nature of nagging self-doubt, or, as you may know it, "writer's block." The term is misleading. It lends self-doubt a calamitous air, as if it were an affliction descending on an unfortunate few instead of a common, self-generated occurrence—so common, in fact, that it's surprising there isn't a compulsory vaccine for teenagers. Though no cure exists, you can still capably treat the symptoms. You were published in an anthology—that's a start. Get off the bench.

I would like to thank the entire staff of the Alliance for Young Artists & Writers for the opportunity to undertake a very enviable job: to live in New York City and read the fantastic work of teenagers from across the nation. More specifically, my heartfelt thanks go out to Bryan Doerries, Lisa Feder-Feitel, Scott Larner and Alex Tapnio—without their guidance, patience, and occasional tea parties this book would not exist. I would also like to thank my family for simply being themselves, the Ethiopian farmer who first discovered coffee, Justin Beltz, for his candor, and—perhaps most importantly of all—Scott Gould, Cynie Cory, George Singleton, and everyone else I encountered at the South Carolina Governor's School for the Arts and Humanities who irrevocably changed my life (this means you, Third Floor Quad).

—Temnete Sebhatu

Temnete Sebhatu received the Nonfiction Portfolio Gold Award and a $10,000 scholarship from the Alliance for Young Artists & Writers in 2007. She selected all the works featured in this anthology. Temnete will be a sophomore at Wesleyan University in 2008, where she will be studying the cracks in her ceiling.

A MESSAGE FROM THE NATIONAL COUNCIL OF TEACHERS OF ENGLISH

The Best Teen Writing of 2008 is the sixth annual installment featuring works selected from national award recipients of The Scholastic Art & Writing Awards of 2008.

The National Council of Teachers of English acknowledges the dedication and passion of every student who submitted an entry to The Scholastic Art & Writing Awards and salutes the 41 students whose work was ultimately published. You'll find this work challenging and provocative—a very good read. By learning to look closely at the world around them, sifting their perceptions, and inviting us to see what they have constructed, these student writers are enriching thousands of readers. At the same time, they have honed valuable skills that can bring them personal satisfaction for a lifetime.

In its Beliefs About the Teaching of Writing (www.ncte.org/about/over/positions/category/write/118876.htm?source=gs), the NCTE asserts that writing is a tool for thinking and that writing grows out of many different purposes. The stories, scripts, essays and poems in this book provide eloquent testimony in support of these beliefs. The clarity and vitality of these texts makes a powerful statement about how even our youngest writers can connect with an audience to make a lasting impression. Teachers, parents, and community leaders will find the intellectual promise of these young authors uplifting, and in some cases, inspirational.

The quality of writing published here is first-rate, and the scope and scale of participation in the 2008 Scholastic Writing Award competition is impressive. This year's awardees can be found in 47 states! Through its distribution of 15,000 free copies of the anthology, Scholastic Inc. is making a powerful statement in support of the skill and subtlety of the newest generation of student writers. As support for the program grows, I look forward to seeing even more students participate in 2009 and encourage schools and affiliated groups across the country to engage more writers by getting behind this special program.

For more than 80 years, classroom teachers have embraced The Scholastic Art & Writing Awards as a way to motivate students, to encourage their creativity and exploration, and to reward those who achieve on the highest level. I believe that the work included in this publication is proof of the powerful impact literacy educators are having even as the modalities of writing and reading are changing in profound ways. I am grateful to The Scholastic Art & Writing Awards for providing the opportunity to recognize outstanding teenage writers and acknowledge the debt we all owe to their teachers for their commitment to students and the craft of writing.

—Kent Williamson
Executive Director,
National Council of Teachers of English

SNAKES AND SPIDERS

 If you're young, something terrible is about to happen to you.

Consider this to be the natural collision between the impulses of childhood and the freedom of adulthood. You'll be free to act on all your desires, and one of them will leave you devastated.

At 18 years old I rented my first apartment, worked two jobs, and saved my money for college. My favorite dessert was cherry pie, so I bought a pie and sat down to eat the entire thing. Not halfway through, I'd eaten the last bite of cherry pie I'd ever want. May you learn this lesson so easily. I didn't. Most of you won't.

You'll find yourself at 19 or 20 or 22 years old addicted to drugs or alcohol. Or pregnant. Or crippled from a car accident, or maybe from a high dive into shallow water. You'll contract herpes or worse. You'll ring up a fortune in credit card debt and find yourself stuck in a terrible job just to pay the interest.

Some version of this will happen to each of you, moving from childhood into adulthood, and you'll have to manage this burden until you die. Of course a baby isn't so terrible, but this is how it will feel: like the end to everything big and bright you imagined would be possible in your life. You'll feel stuck, trapped by your mistake, but it's what you do with this situation that will save you. The truth is every phase of your life will offer some new terror you can't resolve or tolerate.

You might never find someone to love. You might never earn the money to feel secure. You'll fret about not having a child. Then you'll live in terror your child might suffer, might die. Then you'll worry about your parents' health. After all that, you'll find a mole that's changed color. Every year will introduce you to some new monster you can't vanquish.

That's the secret joy of writing—and dancing, painting, composing, acting. You have a way to explore those worst fears, really depict those worst-case scenarios, and exhaust your emotional reaction. By writing about those fears—of violence or car accidents or illness— you'll have permission to research what you fear the most. You'll meet real people who've suffered and survived what you pray never happens.

In college, I studied a therapy called "flooding," where a patient is forced to confront his or her worst fear. If it's snakes or spiders, the patient is locked into a room filled with snakes or spiders. After the initial horror, that room feels fine. After writing about your worst fear, exploring it from every angle, taking it to every extreme, a writer finds that same reward. Beyond comfort, the snakes and spiders become fascinating, then funny.

Your job as a writer is to trick people into going places they'd never volunteer to explore, and humor is a great bait. It will even trick you into going deeper into your own dark fears of death, loss, humiliation, pain. That said, don't write to be liked. Instead, write about what people aren't ready to love. Eventually they will love you, but that's never the point. When disaster does arrive in your life, use it. Those snakes and spiders? Tell a joke at their expense. Embrace them. Then, sell the bastards.

—Chuck Palahniuk

Chuck Palahniuk is best known for his novel Fight Club. *He is also the author of the bestselling novels:* Choke, Lullaby, Survivor, *and* Diary, *and a collection of essays,* Stranger Than Fiction. *In 2007 he delivered a memorable keynote address to The Scholastic Art & Writing Awards winners at Carnegie Hall. He also served as a national juror for The Scholastic Art & Writing Awards of 2008 in the Short Short Story category. His newest novel,* Rant, *was released on May 1, 2007. Palahniuk currently resides in Vancouver, Washington.*

PORTFOLIO GOLD AWARDS

GRADUATING HIGH SCHOOL SENIORS MAY SUBMIT A PORTFOLIO OF 3–8 WORKS FOR REVIEW BY AUTHORS, EDUCATORS, AND LITERARY PROFESSIONALS. WINNERS OF THE GENERAL WRITING PORTFOLIO AND NONFICTION PORTFOLIO GOLD AWARD RECEIVE $10,000 SCHOLARSHIPS.

HOMETOWN HARMONICS

EMMA MORRISON, 17

SAINT ANN'S SCHOOL
BROOKLYN, NY
TEACHERS: MATTHEW LAUFER, MARTIN SKOBLE,
  ELIZABETH BOSWORTH

Sometimes, on hot milky mornings, my mother would take me to dive off of the wharf. It was a forbidden place, but on days when the pump had dried out from the fever-hot dank air, children were lowered, legs swinging and arms stretched from their mothers' white-knuckled grip, into the oil-dyed water. The wharf was a quiet place, guarded by the beheaded cylinders of once-functioning docks that poked up through the licking water. There was one pier left, its surface like a small child's gap-toothed smile, wiggle edged, missing key planks we had to skip over. This is the pier from which our mothers would hang us, dipping our pinked and burned skin into the thick water for quick moments of relief.

The wharf is private government property; a slit in rusted chicken wire, hidden by one of the forests of weeds, dandelions, and razor grass that are all too familiar to our town, granted us entry. The wharf was closed back when smoke had settled over the town and the factory stopped making more, back when the men in the blue plastic hats left, paint started chipping, stores were boarded shut, and a new liquor store opened up.

Our town was and is poor, with sewage tanks brewing in the Southern heat and our three churches each full on weekends. We have four liquor stores and a bus stop to take children to the school in another town, a better town, many miles away. The bus stop is also how we escape this place, never to return to the sun-broiled summers and the swollen-belly children. It isn't easy to leave, to take the first steps away from the houses set back from the gritty roads packed hard from bare-foot stomps and pickup truck tire rumbles.

Our house was quiet, an enclave away from the one-street town; hidden behind tall dying trees with peeling bark and sickly leaves, shading and sheltering our small family from the sun and the sadness. We were our own tribe of three: three women, three girls, always at war, always together. Left to ourselves for much of the time while our mother was working at the factory three towns, four hours away, my sister and I would wax rhapsodic about the day that the bus would take us far away from the stifling summers and our teenage troubles. She wanted to go north, to the bright lights of New York City, and be a waitress. I wanted to travel across the world alone.

Life was slow in our town. Separated from the world, not many people read the newspapers and even fewer watched the news. Days were centered around lawn chairs and shade, any escape from the Southern heat to which we never became accustomed. When the factory left, our town began dying. Houses slowly emptied of life, left behind as wooden skeletons without doors or windows or fixtures, stripped of use, place-holders for memories. The clothing of neighbors and ourselves became yellowed, old, and torn, stretching across our chests as each year we grew bigger. And every year, we would watch some of a generation climb onto the bus as it rolled through our town, never to return, never to look back.

But the town had a hold on people. Something about the over-grown shrubs and the rusted mailboxes, the colicky children, and the wearisome weather was impossible for many to leave. We were born into this dusty chestnut earth, raised to chew wheat stalks and save our school lunches for dinner, to sneak into the wharf in the dark hours of the night to cool our blistered, stretching skin, to sit on the side of the main road and watch the buses sway by, taking others far from home.

My sister writes me letters these days. She is a waitress, not in New

York City, but in Detroit, and she is happy with her life. I think about her a lot, when I am riding the bus with my mother and my neighbors to a better town, to the factory where we will always work. I don't write her back that often, there isn't much to tell except to help her remember. Small things change—we painted our house and I learned how to knit—but the town is still poor, and on hot mornings, the mothers dip their children, legs flailing, into the cooling water off the edge of the wharf.

SUNDAYS ARE FOR LOVERS
EMMA MORRISON

I have told everyone but Noah Leavitt that I love him. The last people in the world to know, besides him, were my mother and father, but I think that that is normal because most 13-year-old girls don't confide the inner workings of their most complicated hearts to dear old mum and pop. I told them at dinner tonight that I was madly in love, and the reaction I received was to be expected, unexpressive and unconcerned, the two facial expressions I am usually awarded when I attempt to involve them with the tumultuous turns of my passions and romances. My parents tell me that I am too young, that I will grow out of these preoccupations, that they are only infatuations infecting the actively pubescent. I tell them that they are infected with the classic middle-aged suburban couple affliction of repressed emotion and one too many soggy tuna casseroles. And when my mother does not show offense at my onslaught on her mediocre cooking, I have proven my point.

We buy our tuna from Noah Leavitt. His father owns the delicatessen in our neighborhood, the purveyor of gefilte fish and Oreo cookies. I like to shop in their store on Sundays, when Noah is working the counter and I am buying my favorite Bubblicious gum. Noah is an Orthodox Jew. He attends the Yeshiva of Flatbush School. He wears his yarmulke tilted as jauntily as a yarmulke could be worn, his pais are bouncy but not overly curled, and his tallisim swish sensually as he types into the old cash register with the flip card numbers. I imagine that he wears his thick, military green, coke-bottle glasses because he has injured his eyes poring over the Torah in the dark of night and that the thin, sparse strip of hair above his lips is unshaven because of a religious obstacle.

But for Noah, even during the heat of August, I always wear long skirts and turtlenecks on Sundays. I comb my unruly hair and tuck it behind my ears like I imagine a good Orthodox girl does, I wipe off my Scarlett O'Hara lipstick and Marilyn Monroe mole, and I lower my unmascaraed eyes demurely. I have a taste for dramatics and acting is my forte. Three weeks ago, when I was paying for one jar of dill pickles, one pint of kosher vanilla ice cream, and one package of everything-flavored flatbread, Noah, his dry, crackled hand resting on the moist, perspiring ice cream, asked me my name. I looked up into his muddy-brown eyes, smiled, and lied. I said, "My name is Ruth, and I go to Ramaz."

My name is Angela and I go to St. Mary's, which is the all-girls Catholic prison where we are forced to garb ourselves in unflattering navy sacks that mortifyingly have our school logo, a cross, embroidered across the entire backside. My best friend Samantha, who is three years older that me and just like a cliché because she smokes cigarettes in the women's bathroom in the basement and wears heavy green eyeliner and teases her hair, tells me that when guys turn around to see her so-called "bubble butt," the only thing they can see is the flaming cross that is just like a chastity belt. The nuns who drill our classes into a dazed monotonous state of sitting call me precocious and unfortunately thespian, unappreciative of my embellishments of the weekly Bible recitation. Nor do they enjoy the trills and flavor that I find necessary to incorporate into our choral classes and concerts. But when I went to Synagogue for our family friend's daughter's Bat Mitzvah, the cantor seemed to go out on a limb and sing the Jewish songs exactly as he wanted.

■

My first unrequited love was Bobby Flaherty, the freckle-faced Irish boy who was in my Sunday morning gymnastics class. We both took rhythmic gymnastics at the neighborhood fitness center, and I was always jealous of Bobby because he had the nicest silk ribbon wands and the better Michael Jackson dance routine. Our teacher, Ms. Bradley, always told us that with practice we might one day be as good as Bobby, her star pupil, who had won the gold medal in a county rhythmic gymnastics competition against adults. Four years older than me, Bobby had an uneven crop of light tangerine hair and so many freckles that his face also appeared to be almost entirely orange. He used to wear black leggings and tight white T-shirts that would become see-through and moist from perspiration in the chest area after an hour of practicing jazz slides. Last August, I decided that he was going to be my until-death-do-us part when he complemented me on my left wrist ribbon flutter. The next month I saw him kissing another boy.

Noah Leavitt used to take Lee Kaufman to the movies and for ice cream every weekend, until Lee broke his heart and left Noah for her rabbi's son. I know this because of my next-door neighbor, Georgie, whom I used to love too, until he became actively pubescent, which made his voice start to crack and his skin bubble sorely. Also, he told me that he thought that I was really strange. Georgie said that he went with his asinine older brother Jason to buy beer from Noah's father's store and Noah was sobbing and dripping all over the old-fashioned cash register and the selection of candy. Jason and Georgie found a sliver of emotion in their cold, heartless bodies and took pity on the devastated Noah. I had never noticed Noah before. His pale, puffy face was usually hidden behind the rows of powdered vitamin supplements and chewy fruit pastilles, but when I heard of the romantic tragedy that had befallen a fellow adventurer on the journey of inamorata, I went to comfort him and I met my soul mate.

I want to be Jewish. I want a set of strict rules that have been followed for thousands of years, I want to be a survivor of persecution, I want a personal connection to Israel and Palestine, and I want to be proud of my heritage. I want Jesus and Moses, and seven days of presents in December. I want latkes and Manischewitz. I want to have 13 perfect Jewish children. I want to go to Ramaz and be Ruth and never be called obnoxiously precocious but instead gifted and talented. I want my parents to appreciate my eccentricities and my dramatics. I want someone to be in love with me for once. I want to be Mrs. Leavitt the rabbi's wife and the perfect wife and the perfect Jew.

TO LILY SPELLMAN
EMMA MORRISON

I might miss you, Lily "Penis Breath" Spellman. I might just miss you. You sat in front of me in our math class today, and the boys behind us whispered the entire time about the thong that glowed against the pale fat that rolled over your too-tight jeans. Part of me wanted to tell them that you had pulled it out of those pants at the beginning of class, that I saw you do it, that you wanted them to see and that you wanted them to talk about you. I noticed that you have split ends in your skunk-like highlighted hair and a strange mole on the back of your neck.

You do stupid things, Lily, trying to make people talk. You should learn how to stay away from boyfriends, girlfriends too, and tuck that cleavage back into your shirt. But I wonder, Lily, what goes on in that shuttered house at the end of the dried-lawn neighborhood, that shingled chipping house where the men in pickup trucks drop you off and the newspaper boy hears screams in the morning. Lily, are you sad? If so, I can be sad with you. You don't really notice me, but sometimes I notice your mist-fogged eyes, your sad eyes, and how you look startled when you realize that for a moment you allowed yourself to be vulnerable, the kind of naked that you aren't comfortable with. People don't really like you in this school, Lily, but I think that you know that and that makes me sorry. When I was different, when I didn't understand, I didn't like you either, I didn't like the things you did, the way you were. I'm not like you, Lily, I don't like attention, but sometimes I wish that I could be as strong as you pretend to be, the way that you clear hallways and the way that you do the things that you do. You act like you have a tough skin, and maybe sometimes you do, but lately I've been looking at it and touching it and it's not thick enough at all. You have a lot of secrets, Lily, and I wish that I could give you someone to confide in. What happened to you? To make you so seem so callous but be so battered? What goes on inside your house, inside your eyes? Will you remember me when I'm gone? Will they?

You might notice, Lily, when they stop, the little things that I try to do for you. I erase what they write in the bathroom, and I am a barrier behind you in classes, protecting you from their spit-inflected insults, taking them and hurting with them for you. I have sad eyes too, sad eyes that could understand you, but you look through me, not realizing that maybe we could be not so different. I still don't know why I feel for you, Lily. I'm a desk to you, a chair, a pencil, a leaf of paper, an eraser, but I hurt for you and the bruises on your arms. I worry how you will be when I'm gone, your secret guardian angel, but you have a thick skin and I believe you will just continue to do the things that you do, those things that give you nicknames and create giggles in our cramped school hallway. I think that you could really be something, Lily, be someone, but I know you, and you're not the type to leave this town, no matter what it does to you and you do to it. I'm sorry that I have to leave you now, Lily, but it's getting too warm outside. If you had ever turned around in a class, or looked to your left at lunch, you could have seen me and maybe you would have realized what I now know. I hope that you can and that you will change. You're not doing as well as you think that you are; people don't like you, don't understand, and don't want to. I think that I'm going to miss you, Lily Spellman. I really think that I might.

DATE OF RELEASE
JASMINE HU, 16
LYNBROOK HIGH SCHOOL
SAN JOSE, CA
TEACHER: CONNIE WILLSON

It's when the first rays of strange eastern light hit a distant skyscraper that I know this place is no longer mine. I don't recognize its thousand twisting streets that all sound the same, all monosyllabic, all empty. I flinch at this foreign new sun stamped upon jagged steel horizons, this newly acquired dirt beneath my fingernails, at the screeching quality of these sidewalks. My mother told me it would be easy to remember, that it would be like riding a bike after ten years of letting it rust in the garage, but she was wrong. Nothing quite belongs.

I've read up on hutongs for Trivia Bowl. I know that they are relics from the Qing and Ming dynasties, ancient alleyways that sprawl across the city, traversing main streets and shopping malls to intersect at that red-walled, forbidden nucleus. But it is a different thing to see them wake up. When faint red light descends upon pocked walls and broken shingles, the streets stretch their cobblestone spinal cords and mewl softly, a thousand battered, smoke-gray cats. The old women emerge with their chamber pots and shuffle to the public restrooms emanating the unmistakable stench of urine. The merchant rides through the hutong on his bicycle, his deep, braying yells of steamed buns and corn drowning out the creak of bicycle wheels.

Jet lag has kept me up and I'm sitting on bamboo slats in my underwear, trying to ignore the persistent calls of steamed buns and finish *Wuthering Heights* for Trivia Bowl's literature section. It's hot already and this strange blood sun is in my eyes. Soon it will hemorrhage, the harsh scarlet paling to a brittle gray, barely distinguishable from the sky upon which it's superimposed. Soon my grandfather will get up. His hands, bony and graceless, so like my own, will grasp at a bed corner and his spine will unfurl in the already-humid air. He will haltingly make his way to the kitchen to boil a pot of water to make the tasteless porridge that always leaves me hungry, no matter how many bowls I eat. And then my grandmother will awaken to take her place on the black leather sofa. The moment she sees me she will ask me if I want new clothes. She's asked the same question for a week already, even though I've given the same answer each time. I'll finish brushing my teeth with green tea toothpaste in the cramped little bathroom and as soon as I stick my head out she'll accost me from her perch on the black leather sofa with suggestions of skirts and blouses and pants.

I'll always say no. I never mean for her to get that look on her face; I just don't want her money wasted on my awkward breasts and gawky shoulders. I try to say it without a hint of condescension, with no downward tilt to the corners of my lips, but the Mandarin comes out wrong; my voice is exactly the sort that you'd expect from a person who is trying to convince someone that they are not growing old.

This answer will always anger my grandmother. She'll tell me with shaking hands that she would buy me beautiful clothes, not the American crap that I wear. Here, women are fashionable. Don't I trust her? Do I think she is useless?

Today I'm tired and I agree to a pair of shoes. After all, on some days I like my feet; a boy once told me I had cute toes. "What color?" she asks, the turbulence of her features softening. I let her pick.

I don't know what kind of birds they are. Trivia Bowl doesn't have a section on zoology so I never bothered studying birds. They're small and jewel-bright, fluttering, useless. Like the hundred shining baubles my mother and I hung with gritted teeth in an attempt to resemble the kind of families we saw on television, these birds are ornamentation, the sort that are always in cages. There are two of them. They have pert black masks and small beady eyes ringed in blue. They sit in a small, round wooden cage in the corner of the living room. The fan is purposely pointed away from them, my grandfather explains, because they're from the tropics and can't stand too much cold. As I twitch a finger through the cage bars they scatter in a panicked gold and green blur of wings, hopping to the higher bars.

My grandfather comes in with the birdseed, sprinkling the granules of millet and rice into a miniscule tray. They peck eagerly and mindlessly, twin daubs of rainbow gluttony. The tendons in my grandfather's neck lose their tension and stop their minute vibrations, like the slackened strings of a violin. It is then that he turns to me and tells me to put on a pair of sneakers because we are going for a walk. That's his way—brusque, sudden; questions are a waste of saliva. I'm sick of Heathcliff, so I follow without protest. Before we leave my grandfather grabs the birdcage.

"Why are you bringing that?" I ask as I shove my heels into my tennis shoes.

He tells me we're walking the birds. Apparently this is a frequent pastime of the retirees of the city, dating back to the Qing dynasty. The logic is that birds are not supposed to stagnate in some dusty corner of the living room; they are meant to be outside, to be in constant movement, to have the sunlight of their surroundings shift and change. So old men get up every morning at dawn and hook the round wooden cages around the fingers, walking along the winding alleyways, letting their pet finches and sparrows see the cooked yams and crystallized hawthorn berries of street vendors.

We walk through the hutong, passing by the women fanning themselves while sitting on plastic milk crates, the men absorbed in games of Chinese chess. My grandfather greets the ones he knows with an inclination of his hand, causing the birds to scatter in fear every time. Somehow I can't believe that this is an enjoyable experience for them, no matter what Qing traditions dictate. They are jostled about, leaping from bar to bar. They don't pay much attention to the world outside their cage, their small black eyes gazing inward unless a passerby's sleeve happens to brush too close.

Near the mouth of the hutong my grandfather stops at a wall of one of the ancient four-walled courtyards that line the alley. He places the palm of his hand against the crumbling wall, tracing a red spray-painted character that's all angles.

"Chai," my grandfather reads. It means demolish. A hundreds-year-old building, memories slapped to its sides like plaster, is condemned and all the birds can think to do in their cage that hangs from my grandfather's finger is twitter.

Before dinner my grandfather chops up bits of lettuce and carrots for the birds as I try to memorize a Yeats poem for the literature section. Turning and turning in the widening gyre. The falcon—it was a falcon, I'm positive—the falcon cannot hear the falconer. I set the collapsible table with the dishes that my grandfather has cooked, repeating the poem under my breath.

What were the next lines? Things . . . things fall apart, the center cannot hold. As we eat I notice that my grandmother's eyes have acquired the habit of locking onto anything, with an empty persistence. She chews her small pieces of beef and beans, making bovine circles with her lower jaw, bits of spittle dangling from the corner of her mouth. But it's really her eyes that frighten me; though they share the same shape and color, the same wrinkles borne from loud laughter in the corners, they're so different from my mother's.

The center of my mother's eyes lock with fierce purpose. They stare resentfully at me, for what I can never remember, when she tells me how she struggled: struggled when the Cultural Revolution forced her family to the countryside and she had to skin frogs to survive, struggled to get into the top school in the country, struggled her way to America and, when there, struggled to make it in a land where the past is brushed away with last week's Taco Bell enchilada. I can understand my mother's resentment; after all, I am her blurry photo negative, pale and unprocessed. Her without the memories. There's so much of us within each other that aunts and uncles often mistake me for her. I'll pick up the phone and they'll start talking of some problem or some throwaway gossip before realizing that the voice on the other end of the line is not hers. They'll only notice it when they feel the absence of something within my speech, some conviction, some neat alignment of words.

In the past few weeks, three streets down, the demolition teams have destroyed an entire courtyard, spraying thousand-year-old rubble and plaster dust over the cobblestone ground. And my grandmother has been calling me by my mother's childhood nickname.

Things fall apart.

■

We meet other birdwalkers at the park on some days. They are usually toothless old men, faces pleasantly creased and browned, a white nappy fuzz crowning their heads. Once at the park they hang their cages in one long line against the walls of the park so the birds can socialize through the bars. Then they grab long sticks and dip them in buckets of water and practice water calligraphy upon the cement ground, creating transient brush strokes of characters and landscapes. The dominating theme is often birds, birds with flapping wings above reeds, birds skimming sky and water. My grandmother used to draw calligraphy birds with fine horse-hair brushes, each deft flick of her wrist translating into delicate feather and talon. But now her hands shake so much that she can't paint anymore.

According to the birdwalkers, illness can be released through birds. Simply open the cage door and let the birds fly into the open air, taking under their wings the malignant spirits that plague you. "Bird release," one of them says as he suckles hungrily from his cigarette, "is a release of evil, of worry." My grandfather has known of this superstition for quite some time already but he nods his head in thanks. I watch the birdwalkers brush the ground with water, etching smooth lines of upturned wings and claws.

When we make our way back, my grandfather points to a square building opposite the mouth of the hutong. "We were going to go to that hospital," he says. "They could perform an operation on her—drill two holes on the top of the head, connect a live wire. The jolt helps with brain function. But we didn't. It cost too much and she is too proud." He says this with his characteristic unabashed candor, eyes fixed firmly ahead, even bluntly digging a thumb and forefinger into my scalp to illustrate the details of the operation. After a moment he releases his two-digit grip upon my head and says, "You were born there, you know. That hospital."

This is the sort of information that shouldn't matter to me. It's like the photographs of me my mother is intent on keeping, me with the plump cheeks and elfin chin and strange ears, me bundled up for winter, me dancing in a pink cotton dress. "For your memories," she always says, but they're not my memories. I don't remember winter in Shanghai. I don't remember my birth.

I do remember the day when my mother received a phone call in the spring of last year, around the time that my grandmother first requested my grandfather to keep two birds. I am in a conference room that smells of disinfectant, answering question number 47 of the State Trivia Bowl mythology section: Which of the following was the monstrous creature that the King of Crete enclosed within a labyrinth? It is C, Minotaur. I am positive. Janine is doubtful—she thinks Chimera——but I press the buzzer anyway. And as I shout my answer to a string of applause, the phone in our house rings three times before my mother picks it up. (She has been in the shower.) I can imagine her voice, resounding with the confidence I have yet to inherit and then faltering with a low groan.

At the State Bowl we pile into David's car. The team congratulates me, Janine ruffling my hair and offering me a beer. We've always envied Janine because she is the only one of us whose parents leave six-packs out in the open like that. It wasn't so much the taste of beer itself that we hungered for; it was the feel of badass coursing through our bloodstreams, the golden strength of something that could counteract the Friday nights spent memorizing minutiae in our rooms.

"Glad you didn't listen to me," Janine says to me as I sip from the can, licking the edge of the steel, my nose wrinkling at the shock of alcohol.

"You were great." David turns from the front seat and grins, and I feel the beer coursing up my nostrils and my ears and my fingers, the tips of which seem to glow with warmth. I say thanks, and as he leans over he spills a few drops from his can onto my turquoise flip-flops. Before I can say anything he conjures up some Kleenex and wipes my feet.

"You've got cute toes," he says, before turning around and starting the ignition.

■

There's really no protocol to follow when someone gets Alzheimer's. Births and deaths are simple—congratulations or condolences—little ambiguity to the natural rhythms of celebration and mourning. But there's little to offer someone whose mental faculties are being systematically chipped away like crumbling plaster and rotten wood.

The only thing we could do, my mother decided, was to play Ariadne, to offer some sort of fine golden thread for the darkness. So when David dropped me off in front of my house, when I returned with my gleaming state trophy and a mouthful of Winterfresh to hide the smell of beer on my breath, my mother told me that my grandmother had Alzheimer's and asked me if I wanted to go to Beijing in the summer.

If only understanding were a light switch. If only there were something in our genetic code of bundled double helixes that could store our memories, contain them so that we could possess all the stories that we have in our blood. I've always been obsessed with memorizing but I can't remember what I never knew. And I don't know my grandmother, not really. I can't recall the first time she felt the white void of snow crunching beneath her feet or that night when she went fishing, plopping each silver fish into a bucket, sleek bodies like captured moonlight. I can't know what she's forgetting.

"Sure," I say. "I'll go to Beijing."

And so I'm in Beijing. I'm in an apartment so humid that the green wallpaper seems to stick to my skin. I'm sitting at the collapsible table, the birds chattering in the background, as my grandfather pulls out a newspaper and a dog-eared calendar. As we stab at dates, consulting the paper's weather forecast, my grandmother sinks into her black leather sofa, engrossed first in soap operas, then in shampoo commercials, then the situation in the Middle East. As the over-lipsticked announcer talks about Mahmoud Ahmadinejad, whose name I barely recognize when translated into Chinese, the three of us establish a date of release, the same date as my flight back to California.

■

The shoes are hideous. They're yellow and I've never liked yellow, especially not this particular shade of cheap cheddar. They've got clunky heels that I could never walk in and some sort of large, plump polka-dotted bow at their tips, too exuberantly tacky to be ironic. I slip my feet into them while sitting on the corner of the bed that I've made mine for the past month. I'm proud of the indentation of my body upon that rock-hard mattress. It's nice to leave a mark.

On the wall of the room hangs a photograph of my grandmother and grandfather in their 20s. I haven't paid much attention to it in the last few weeks, just noted that they were indeed my grandparents, probably at the beginning of their careers at the Foreign Ministry, young and smiling. But now I look at it and drink the details in. My grandfather has a hand barely raised in greeting toward the unseen picture-taker, his smile frozen in mid-laugh. My grandmother's eyes, so like my mother's, burn like an architect's might before a set of blueprints as she places a hand on her swollen stomach.

She pads softly into my room, finding me with those clownish yellow shoes upon me feet. It's one of her better days and she smiles at the shoes complacently, reveling in I-told-you-so. She tells me she bought them because they reminded her of a dress she used to have when she was young, when she went to her first dance at college and danced with a boy who would recite Tang poetry to her. "Li Po," she said. "Or was it Du Fu? I can't remember."

I've tried to memorize Tang poems with strangely wrought titles like "On the Moonlit Precipice of the Three Gorges, Thinking of Shang" before but I can't read Chinese well and so much is bent and twisted in translation. My grandmother rests her head on my shoulder as we both pant in the humidity, her head leaving a patch of sweat on my shirt but neither of us shifts in discomfort.

"You've always been a good daughter to me," my grandmother says, holding my hand in hers. "When you were born in Germany, Fraulein Fischer next door sent over one of her cakes and told me that you were such a beautiful baby, because you were golden, golden like the sun."

I tell her I love the shoes, I don't think I'm lying. As we sit motionless in the morning humidity the fan hums and the birds continue their chirping.

■

On the date of release my bags are packed, waiting expectantly in the corner of the green living room. The birds are next to them. They have grown fat with days of gorging on millet. I'm worried that they won't be able to fly away; they seem to pant more than usual after a bout of fluttering. Or maybe it's just the heat.

My grandfather hooks the birdcage with his forefinger. The birds think it's just any normal day, just another walk around the hutongs and the park to sit with cigarette men and other birds, the same jostling, the same brushed sleeves. They aren't expecting liberation.

We step outside, all three of us. My grandmother walks first with her small, mincing steps, then my grandfather, birdcage in hand. I follow them both. We make our way past the apartment complex, past the mimosa trees that line the hutong and scatter pink blossoms across its sidewalks. We wind past the rubble of the destroyed courtyard and ignore the clangs of the bulldozer, ignore the spray-painted signs of condemnation and focus our eyes on the dusty center of things.

At the park we find a secluded spot underneath the junction of two willow branches. The cage is placed on the grass. The two birds are unusually quiet—perhaps they sense something missing within the rhythm of our usual walks. We are still, our breaths evaporating mid-esophagus. Then my grandfather opens the cage.

The birds rattle out with the tenacity of escaped convicts, never even daring to look back. We expect them to land in the willows but they don't. They keep flying, soaring faster and faster until we can't keep track of where they are or where they're going. They are far above ground now, somewhere with a cool wind, and we three, their once-captors, are losing the significance of oppression with every foot in gained altitude, turning first into dwarves and then specks and then invisible altogether. From their view the hundreds of thousands of twisting labyrinthine hutongs writhe and shimmer under the harsh sun. In a few hours I'll see the same scene from the window of an airplane but for now I cling to the wrinkled paper hands of my grandmother and grandfather, wondering if they too feel something shifting and locking into place in the pit of their stomachs.

"Isn't this better than two holes in my skull?" my grandmother says, her face tilted skyward. "Cheaper and easier on the eyes." Slowly, we make our way back.

NAMES
JASMINE HU

At 8 a.m., over their breakfasts—coffee for him, oranges for her—just as Vincent fills in seven across (five-letter word for a symbol of Greece: olive) on the daily crossword, April asks, And what if it was a boy? Because, after all, the receptionist at work had seen the way her stomach stretched under green cashmere and after 17 grandchildren brought into the world, mark her words, it was going to be a boy. Though they maintained that he wanted a boy to play football with and she wanted a girl to not mock Sandra Bullock films, neither of them cared much either way, too thrilled and frightened by the prospect of this new and fragile extension beyond themselves; it was, she would say much later, as if they were on the edge of some great precipice.

He looks up from ten down. "How about Chip?"

"Chip. Like, Pringles, a wood chipper."

"No, that's woodchopper."

"Either way," she says, lack of coffee drawing harsh lines of morning light across her face, "it's a pretty shitty name, like one of those male strippers at that thing? What do you call them—y'know, with the bows around their necks like they're going to burst?"

"Chippendales," he says. "I still don't get why you don't like Vincent."

"Too confusing. Who would I be talking to?"

"Hasn't bothered my family for seven generations." He uses the classifieds to wipe away a small coffee puddle. "In any case, if we take any longer our parents will feel the need to provide input."

April picks up the drenched rag and sniffs it longingly. "We should name him Juan Valdez. God, I miss caffeine. And I already told my mother she could pick a Chinese middle name. Vin, what if it comes out looking like a sea monkey?"

By now he is acclimated to the constant bend and sway of her thoughts, strange meandering creatures with tadpole tails. But he sees the way that her pale, swollen fingers are stained with newspaper ink, how her forehead is creased with slight shadow, and knows that she has trouble sleeping at nights for that new sense of purpose in her abdomen. He squeezes his hand around her fingers—she couldn't even take off her wedding ring, and so it stays, digging gently into her— and kisses the shadow of her forehead. "Sea monkeys," he says into her hair. "I never could figure it out. What the hell were those things, anyways?"

■

She remembers how, when she first got engaged, her parents never said anything. Her friends had oh April-ed and squawked of the white male patriarchy, of media brainwashing, of racial and cultural fetishes and many other things that she could laugh at now. Back then, though, she had been indignant, telling them they'd read too many Amy Tan novels, that they weren't about to reduce her engagement to one. But her parents had never said anything. "It was your eyes," her mother later said to April. "Same glint I felt in mine an ocean and 50 years past. People did not like it when the poet's daughter and the wealthy landlord's son got married, but it happened. Same eyes."

Her mother's voice meets her over the phone now. "Here, I've mailed you a list of Chinese names. If your father had been here he would have come up with better things. Always had a way with words."

Instinctively, April winces at the dead leaves rattling out of the receiver and draws a little farther away from her young husband's arm. She can see her mother sitting in the corner of the black leather sofa, making room for the ghost of her husband, still prodigious in death. It didn't seem fair. "Ma, why don't we name the kid after Dad?"

"The Chinese," Ma says, "don't do that. Names are never to be recycled. That would mean bad luck."

"All the eldest sons in Vincent's family are named Vincent," April says.

"Really?" her mother asks, incredulous, "His father's name?"

"Vincent."

"His grandfather's name?"

"Vincent."

"His grandfather's father's name?"

"Vincent. And the one before that—Vincent."

Ma mutters something meant only for her husband's ghost.

"She wants to know," April whispers, hand over receiver, her laughter tickling Vincent's ear, "why Americans are so weird."

■

He likes listening to her speak on the phone to her mother, making those hard syllables that fall like rain. When they had been dating she tried to teach him some Chinese, giving him a book of four-character idioms. Vincent never was one for languages—he scraped through high school Spanish by buying his teacher some burritos and a Pablo Neruda anthology—and eventually they gave up with the Chinese but still kept the book to laugh at how lengthy stories of men waiting for rabbits under trees, ships flaming, and elephants being weighed managed to condense themselves into four characters that did not make up the length of a thumb.

The list comes and she sticks it under his nose, as if the spiders and squat boxes that stomp their way across the page meant anything to him. "What are they?" he asks.

"Names," she says. And she starts reading them off—the same hard syllables with tones pushing themselves up and down like a seesaw.

"What do they mean?"

"Well," she purses her lips, "it's a little hard to translate. Chinese names aren't like Matthew or Joshua—they're more like . . . ideas. So this would be—I think—Pensive Lamb. And that would be Clear Thought." And before he can be too stunned at the idea of having a son named Pensive Lamb, she tells him how characters work by generation, how specific ones are passed down through the family tree like heirlooms.

"But not complete names," he says.

"The verdict is that we just don't do that. Bad luck. Do you want to curse our kid to a lifetime of redundancy and cyclical misfortune?"

"Cyclical misfortune?"

She shrugs. "What my mom says."

"So you absolutely rule out Vincent?"

"Well," she says slowly, "you know I don't really believe that stuff. But cyclical misfortune is pretty damning, and one Vincent is probably enough for me, and after all it's a matter of heritage, isn't it?"

He nods and rolls over. Before he falls asleep, he remembers how his father would always tell him to take pride in those seven letters that had survived three wars and countless women and their pasta, how his mother had given him an old set of spoons with that name inscribed on them when they had gotten married. But, as he watches the rise and fall of her stomach, outlined by moonlight, his last conscious thought is that there are things beyond wars and pasta and spoons.

On the other side of the bed, she is still awake, feeling as if they had somehow had a silent argument.

In the morning she unpeels a dream about a guy she used to date from her eyelashes and scrutinizes it through the morning light from the window. He had been a writer—nice guy but he saw symbolism everywhere—flowers couldn't bloom without fear of being compared to nipples or virginity or something, birds couldn't so much as move a feather without being hope in souls or far-flung liberation—and one night he told her that her hair was like the wings of night when it just wasn't. There were clearly more split ends than stars. That's when she had said to him that sometimes a cigar was just a cigar. In her dream she had said that again to him: a cigar is just a cigar.

She sits up and listens to the perfect orchestrations of their fluttering breaths. "Sometimes," April says to her still-sleeping husband, "a cigar is just that. And sea monkeys are a breed of shrimp. I'm not giving anything up, not really, and neither are you. We're just making something new, that's all. I mean, a name's important and culture's important but we're not going to be having a bundle of names or a bundle of culture. We're having a baby, a baby to be named Vincent Clear-Thought Sea-Monkey or something else ridiculous." With a yawn she falls asleep.

At eight a.m. April and Vincent have the same dream, one that they both forget by noon, in which they wait under a tree for a rabbit but instead a child falls like fruit, warm and full of new life.

SPAM MAIL
JASMINE HU

The Poet, somewhere in that no-man's-land between the two big ones of 39 and 49, hair graying at the temples (but you wouldn't know because he rectifies this once a week with Clairol number 507), a type-one diabetic who always carries a sugar packet from 1975 in his wallet, an accomplished writer of five anthologies and several poems in *The New Yorker*, the winner of the National Book Award for Poetry and a rumored frontrunner for this year's Pulitzer, currently sitting with the talk show host on a plush velvet couch that has graced the asses of somebodies and nobodies and anybodies alike, is a man who values consistency and always gives the same answer.

"I get it from issues of human identity and the anachronism of modern man. I like to juxtapose things—completely unrelated things—until it gets to the point of absurdity and then it becomes relevant, because as humans we do this too—we struggle to forge identities in this absurd, absurd way." The Poet has everything pitch-perfect by now, the hand motions, the slight hesitations, the abstractions and permutations and constant regurgitations. The talk show host nods and smiles brilliantly, remarking how she just loved his poems. He doesn't really know why he's on this show. The women in the audience are nice, motherly types who could clearly care less and would much rather see the guy from *Titanic*.

It's backstage that he's allowed to wipe the sweat and makeup from his brow and melt a little, away from the strong glare of the TV set lighting. He pulls out his BlackBerry—it was strange how everyone seemed to peg poets as automatic Luddites, like poetry was analogous to cave painting and quiet hermitage, when in reality he liked his iPod as much as any technological lemming—and checks his e-mail. Twenty new spam messages. Good. He puts the BlackBerry into his pocket and gives himself an insulin shot with the seasoned efficiency of someone who had almost died from a sugar packet in 1975 and is determined never to repeat that particular experience. He likes surviving—after all, that's why he's on a talk show.

Before the host can snag him and stuff him with complimentary bagels and muffins while waxing lyrical about how much she loves his poetry, he leaves the building, dashing across the street to a dingy little café. It isn't a particularly stylish café; it reeks of stale coffee and faux-beatnikism with its framed photos of Jack Kerouac next to its automatic blenders, its quotes about the best minds of my generation hanging on scarlet walls as teenagers "dude" and "whatever" their way through their lattes.

This place seems to be the watering hole of the teenage social periphery. These are not the cheerleaders or even the elegantly jaded urban cynics; these are the ones who name their graphing calculators, who don't understand that bangs need to be washed, the ones whose faces are such hot spots of dermatological activity that you might think they were the meeting points of the Atlantic and Pacific tectonic plates.

It's Open Mike Night at this little beatnik café, and one by one the ghostly apparitions filter in, bits of sodium streetlight still clinging to their shoulders or the gloss of their hair. The Poet knows that the best idea is probably to run out of the room screaming, never looking back—he's tasted the strange aspartame and plaster of teenage poetry before and it's an experience he's not intent on repeating. But the Poet stays put, sipping at his macchiato even though there's nothing left in his cup but dregs of foam. His limbs seem to grow heavier under the wooden table that has accumulated dozens of carved initials and confessions of unrequited love. For a minute he wonders if something hasn't been slipped into his drink, maybe a few dashes of something alcoholic.

A girl gets up and recites a poem about her dead grandfather. It's shit, the kind of rhythmic sing-song thing you get in chain e-mails that tell you to pass it on to all your friends or else your grandfather will die of a stroke too, but the Poet claps as hard as anyone as the girl totters off the stage. He orders another macchiato, hoping that if there was alcohol last time they'd take the trouble to slip some more in.

They seem to get better as the night progresses, or maybe he's just getting acclimated to the evening. The broken glass hearts and bleeding wrists and bright green orbs that connect with mascara-lined brown ones don't make him wince inwardly anymore; they've even gained a sort of repetitive dignity, Homeric epithets of rosy-fingered Dawn and wine-dark seas for the braces-and-lip-gloss set. The Poet gets through two particularly painful poems by a pudgy brunette about a bad breakup and a good hook-up, respectively, without as much as a hint of a knitted brow. He deems this progress and checks his BlackBerry. Twenty-five new spam messages. Good.

Then a boy with glasses and a checked collared shirt gets up, all legs and trembling hands. He's so fragile under the stage lights—his pale skin seems to glow painfully and for a moment the Poet wonders if it's an instance of divinity or albinism. The boy's lips part with a frail rattling honesty, colorless leaves crushed under a thousand callous feet. He squints at the crumpled piece of binder paper in his hands and recites a poem, a real poem, something about the spray of the sea as his mother makes tea in her kitchen, some mention of gleaming teapots and lost steam, some scent of salt, some turned-away faces, a silence at the dining table as the tea is poured. The Poet's BlackBerry is forgotten and he almost shatters his cup of macchiato upon the café's beaten hardwood floor. It isn't genius, not yet anyways, but it's decidedly something. The whole room smells of sea salt as the boy's words linger and reverberate in the air. Now, the Poet decides, would be a good time for him to leave.

But just as he steps out onto the sidewalk, exposing himself to the harsh sodium streetlights, he feels a tap on his left shoulder and spins around to see the boy. He's thinner and paler up close—his glasses are slipping from the bridge of his nose from the sweat of the stage and the yellow glare of sodium engulfs his slight form whole. There's something broken about him, with his too-long fingers and elephantine flapping ears. The Poet pegs him at 16, quiet and unloved by the female of the species. He wants to tell the boy not to worry, that poetry gets all the chicks later on in life, but he doesn't.

"Are you the Pulitzer guy?" the boy asks. Offstage his voice is shrunken and desiccated.

The Poet is surprised. In his four years of literary prominence he'd only been recognized two times before this. Poems don't come with faces; that was part of their appeal. "Not yet," the Poet says. "But yes, I'm that poet."

"Oh," the boy says. He doesn't pretend to like the Poet's poetry, doesn't give him empty compliments about their absurd imagery that he's heard a million times before, and for this the Poet is thankful. But then he licks his leaf lips and makes the mistake of asking The Question, the same question Oprah and a thousand others had asked under the glare of TV lighting.

"Say, if you don't mind telling me, what's your inspiration?"

The old empty rattle on human identity and absurdist juxtaposition lingers at the tip of the Poet's tongue, tickling his palate, ready to be expulsed at the first sign of stimulus. But for some reason it doesn't come out, some neurons refrain from firing, the action potential is truncated at mid-breath. Maybe it's the soft fragility of this boy, so thin you could almost see his bones or at least imagine that you saw them superimposed upon his pale, pale skin. Maybe it's the five possibly spiked macchiatos or the sodium streetlights. But in any case the Poet doesn't speak his old worn speech and instead takes out his BlackBerry.

"Spam e-mail," the Poet says without a hint of embarrassment, showing his bulk folder on the screen. "They use random word generators for the subject lines, so you get stuff like rudimentary Sasquatch, non-recognition panoptic, leonine salmon, that sort of thing. And there's a music and a careful serendipity to them. I'm not a poet like you—in fact I'm quite the fraud. I just collect spam e-mail and string it together with some sense to counter the nonsense and there you have it. Critical acclaim and cash and talk of Pulitzers."

The boy seems shattered. The Poet knows he would have preferred the absurdist rant. But the boy is truth and that lie would have splintered his fragile bones into a thousand unidentifiable pieces, and though the Poet is capable of a good many things, splintering the boy is not one of them. In the darkness illuminated only by sodium streetlight, the Poet walks away. When he reaches the bus stop he gives himself another insulin shot and checks his BlackBerry—29 spam messages. Good.

It's only when the bus driver starts the engine that the Poet realizes he forgot to tell the boy to keep writing.

■

When the Poet enters his apartment, the woman named Naomi is perched atop their leather sofa, smoking a cigarette and painting her left pinky toe with clear polish. The Poet, after a hasty greeting, goes to get himself an egg sandwich and sits across from her, watching her meticulously dab the polish across her cuticles as she unconsciously draws in and expels cigarette smoke, sending twisting tendrils of gray around his head. The Poet doesn't understand the point of clear polish but the woman named Naomi says it's the best kind so he doesn't argue.

The Poet keeps the woman named Naomi around because there is nothing poetic about her. She has inoffensively brown hair and a placid character and plain eyes with no secret depths and a name that nothing rhymed with, except perhaps sigh oh me. When around the woman named Naomi, the Poet never feels moved to write odes to her forgettable plain face or her habit of dressing in the same drab olives and browns of their apartment so that her limbs and torso seem to meld seamlessly with the environment, and that was the way he liked it.

On some nights the woman named Naomi wants to know what his inspiration is, and he would mutter without hesitation that his inspiration was human identity and the anachronism of modern man and, with the slightest pause, "my love for you, of course." Other nights the woman named Naomi would sulk and wonder why she kept the Poet if he wrote no love poetry and demand a poem for herself and herself only, no rudimentary Sasquatches there. And so the poet, eyes half-closed from the weight of dreams, would mutter some nonsense about Naomi, how you make me sigh oh me, oh try oh me, oh me, and the woman named Naomi would be content and he would roll over and they would both sleep until the sun stroked their bedsheets with cold light, their legs crossing and mingling in a sort of silent frigid aubade.

■

"I used to think my mother was an outlaw," the Poet says to her, words blurred by egg sandwich. "She had a big library full of books, and the books all had different names written inside. I thought she stole them from people."

"Did she?" Naomi says uninterestedly.

"No, she wasn't an outlaw, she was a librarian. She took all the rejected book donations home, so we'd have copies of completely inappropriate books like the illustrated Kama Sutra."

The woman named Naomi doesn't look at him, but the words "You aren't that good in bed" are stamped brazenly across her wrinkled brow. "How was the show?"

"Good," the Poet says. "They gave me free bagels."

The Poet doesn't love the woman named Naomi but he knows he thoroughly needs her and he knows that's stronger. Right now as she paints over her toenails and sucks on her cigarette she is an Edward Hopper painting without the stark lyricism. Her gaze is focused utterly inwards, the wrinkles of her crushed satin camisole perfect facets of kitchen light. He needs the woman named Naomi because she doesn't look up when he enters the door anymore, because the woman named Naomi couldn't tell good poetry from bad if her life depended on it, because one strap of her crushed satin camisole is slipping past her shoulder but she doesn't stop painting her toenails a color no one else can see or letting out breath after breath of smoky air.

That night, they slip into bed and as their feet search for each other's warmth the woman named Naomi demands a poem. The Poet doesn't feel like writing another sigh oh me oh me, so he tries to repeat the boy's poem to her. But it's late and he can hardly remember the words, the words that seemed to click into place when the boy read them, something about teapots and seashores, mothers and fathers, love as cold as the tea she pours. But in the end it doesn't matter that he skips lines and forgets phrases because the woman named Naomi is already fast asleep, her right foot curled around his left leg. For a moment during this two-person somnambulistic tango he can't tell which limb is his.

In the morning the Poet sees that the woman named Naomi has disentangled herself from him and left for work, the sheets cold and bright where she would have been. The Poet showers and eats breakfast before giving himself a routine insulin injection and checking his e-mail. He refreshes his BlackBerry twice in disbelief when he sees the number, but there it is, blatant and irrefutable. Zero spam messages.

∎

He checks throughout the day, constantly consulting the BlackBerry, daring the number to change. It never does and droplets of panic trickle slowly into his lungs, suffocating him with an unreasonable drowning madness. It was just spam mail, the Poet tells himself, but he isn't convincing anyone.

When the woman named Naomi comes back from work with a cigarette in hand, tossing off high heels and pantyhose with her customary inward gaze, she tells him she had a spam blocker installed for their e-mails. It cost her $50 dollars and two hours to set up but it's worth it, she says, because she hasn't gotten a single spam message for the entire day. "What about you?" she asks.

"No," he says. "I haven't." She claps her hands in approval over her little act of domesticity, she is a good technological Betty Crocker.

"Is there any way I could have it uninstalled?" the Poet asks, the algae-green muck of panic flooding his chest as the woman named Naomi walks into the kitchen, dragging a stocking on the hardwood floor behind her.

"Uninstalled?" she says. "What for? You said yourself you haven't had a single spam message in the entire day."

"I like getting them," the Poet says, bile blistering and coagulating in his mouth.

"Those things have viruses, you know," she says as she cuts the carrots.

"Look, you don't understand. I use them—I use them to write things."

The woman named Naomi wrinkles her nose sardonically. "I can't remember the last time you wrote about breast enlargement or dating services."

"No," he said with a rattling breath. "The subject lines. I use them in my poems. Rudimentary Sasquatch, non-recognition panoptic, leonine salmon, you know—"

For a moment the woman named Naomi is silent. She puts down her carrot knife, gazes steadily at him with her plain shallow eyes that are no color in particular, and then laughs. She throws back her head and laughs steady, convulsive, inelegant laughter, the hoarse peals tumbling down the side of her face like an avalanche.

"So," she says between gasps, "all this time! All that shit about anachronisms and absurdity, about your careful juxtaposition. All that crap about it being inspired by love. When in reality it was spam. Just spam! When in reality they're all so m—"

■

And then somewhere behind the Poet's tongue a dam breaks and words cascade forward. "Meaningless, yes! Meaningless! But I shaped them into transparent nothings and then I let you pluck whatever damn meaning you wanted from them, you see? I mean, ultimately, can you tell? Do you mind?" The Poet's words run like rivers, they float down the deltas and gorges of his lips, swirling in angry eddies and stagnating furiously within the hollows of his cheeks. The woman named Naomi stops laughing as she drops the carrot she was cutting on the linoleum floor. Suddenly she can't bear to look at him, like he's full of light too harsh for her plain eyes. Like a cigarette, he seems to burn. Like a cigarette, he makes her eyes water.

"We go around looking and looking for this thing, this thing with a capital M, but really it's all just stamps on an envelope, addressed to nowhere in particular. Go ahead, play a game, ask me to find you anything meaningless and I wouldn't know when to stop, from your clear toenail polish or the sugar packet in my wallet—the precious little meaning we hold—it's not there. It's all spam, all generated by some blind God sitting in a room with no windows. And to create meaning? It's too heavy a burden for one poet; I want to let someone else do it. I want the boy under the streetlights to do it. I don't want to write, I don't want to provide meaning like some two-for-one deal; just give me something arbitrary and free from context. I want someone else to do it."

As the woman named Naomi begins to cry from his brightness, something in the Poet's jawbone creaks and locks into place, giving his features a jutting primitive look as he sits down at his desk with a defiant ferocity, a piece of paper in front of him and a pencil in hand. And as the sun sets and the skies darken and the sodium streetlights outside flash their harsh chemical yellow, the apartment echoes with a woman's dry hacking sobs and the furious scratching of pencil upon paper.

THE NUMB ACRE
VIRGINIA PFAEHLER, 17
CHARLESTON COUNTY SCHOOL OF THE ARTS
NORTH CHARLESTON, SC
TEACHER: RENE MILES

I.

I never noticed your stubble
or the pebbled groove of your spine,

but I saw your arm hairs stand up,
soft sentinels moved by the October wind,

my fingers protecting a few of them
as the breeze spun through us, to the harbor.

II.

Water hisses and screams in the kettle.
We mistake it for passion

and imagine ourselves origami:
I crane, you tiger, folding together.

III.

A weight fills the numb acre
between my breasts and my sex,

the erotic slide of your solid language
suddenly absent from my ears.

HAS PASSED
VIRGINIA PFAEHLER

Once, I took raw bacon and made myself a picnic
by the alligator pond, my pink blanket
edged up against the chain-link fence
that separated me from the swampy musk.
I fed the alligator the meat through the fence,
my fingers slimy, but not shivering.
I had dealt with apprehension before,
when I had to clean up the house before my birthday party,
and there were beer bottles stuffed under
the living room chairs and couch cushions.
I felt the cold on my mother's knuckles
as she inhaled and exhaled her past and present,
until I pointed out that only the filter was left.

My mother scared me, cross-legged in front of the TV,
an ashtray dressed with dead cigarettes to the left,
the coffee cup turned over by the cat to the right,
her expression as blank and internal
as the backward pirouette of the moon.

I get up in the middle of the night to creep
toward the bathroom, where nicotine smoke
curls under the door and around the bars
of the birdcage standing outside the bathroom,
uncovered because someone forgot.
She smokes more when her blood flows and is caught.

Her memories surge forward, sway back,
creak fatigue, shed rust flakes in windowsills.
When my father worked the day shift,
when my mother refused to go in at all,
and she slept until my brother and I ran out of things
to tell the women who kept calling, asking,
"May I speak to your mother, please?"

"She's in the shower." "She's gone to get the mail."

"Will you tell her I called?"

"Yes." No. She would worry and tear
at each of her fingernails.
She would rip the cuticles with her teeth clumsily,
clumsy so that you could always see my father's
needled tracks—at first I thought of railroads, now
all I see is a stopped heart, red and raw like a torn pomegranate—
and clumsy so that my mother wiped her tear-wet fingers
on our walls, and my brother and I told people
that our ceiling leaked.

MY FAVORITE PLACES FOR YOUR HANDS

VIRGINIA PFAEHLER

I.
The bone belt of my waist
knows your hands by heart;

Your lifelines fit my veins.
My iliac crest rises for your skin,

is jolted even against your gloves
covered in oil and juice.

II.
Orbicularis oris, the muscle
that makes lips pucker and close,

another ring of soft pink
for you to rest your fingers on.

NOISE
VIVIAN TRUONG, 17

STUYVESANT HIGH SCHOOL
NEW YORK, NY
TEACHERS: EMILY MOORE, ERIC GROSSMAN,
  ANNIE THOMS

A boy asks me why I'm so quiet.
His words are loud and smiling; he
asks me why those
Chinese girls never talk.

And I tell him:

Boy
When I walk I
don't just move upon the earth but
with each step I
make the world

Spin.

Sweetie
when I dance the
soft padding of my feet
makes the ground

Tremor.

Baby
when I sing, my heart throbs
against my voice and I
make the air

Quiver.

And honey
I may not be
the loudest girl you know
and I may not be
one to scream my words
and I may not be
someone who
fills the air with useless babble—
but when I speak, yes,
when I whisper I
make men

Listen.

ORANGES
VIVIAN TRUONG

My brother Jess is a total prick. When Jess was younger, and less of a prick, and when I was younger, and less of a wiseass, we used to spy on the crazy old coot who lived across the alleyway. We'd lean our elbows on the chipping white paint on the windowsill and weave our fingers through the rust-speckled window guards, pressing the tips of our noses against the insect screen and peering into his room.

The crazy old coot still comes to my uncle's store every day. My parents say he's actually 40, maybe 50 years old. But the wrinkles in his face, the gray streaks in his hair, the hobble in his walk make him seem 20 years older.

Once Jess and I were old enough, we started working shifts in the store after school for pocket money. We've gotten used to his presence by now, but that doesn't keep us from staring whenever he comes. We watch him as he runs his wrinkled palms over the cans, fruits, and bags of cookies. He grasps the shelves as he pulls himself across the store, to the box overflowing with oranges. He weighs them in his hands, hands covered in liver-spotted raisin skin and a web of blue veins. He sifts and digs through the oranges, pounds them with his white palms, listening for the juice that fills the pulp inside. The gold band around his fourth finger taps against the pockmarked rinds.

He'd tell us stories, about home and about the owner of the ring. His wife's ring and the clothes he wore were the only things he had left from Beijing. He'd tell us this detail, over and over again: just his wife's ring and the clothes on his back. He'd tell it to us every day as if he was reminding us to brush our teeth. He told us that he wanted to keep the ring warm, as she had always kept it warm. And now his knuckles have grown too large to allow its removal.

We watch as he surfaces with a sallow yellow fruit, an orange that isn't orange. He makes his way to the counter and pulls change out of his tattered silk pockets.

"Why don't you ever buy the freshest ones?" Jess asks. He accepts the payment and places the fruit into a plastic bag. "Why don't you take what you can have?"

The old man doesn't answer. He stares at the ring on his finger. Then he takes the bag, the plastic rustling in his fingers as he walks out of the store.

He'll be thinking of the white tiles on his kitchen floor, of the smell of his wife's hair, of the way the dust swirled and caught the soft golden sunlight beaming through the living room window, of the chubby toddler he dreamed of running in and out of the rooms in his house. Then, of panic, of gunshots, of riot, of the swelling that ballooned in his chest and crowded against his lungs and heart, of the memory of the Styrofoam taste of dry oranges in his mouth.

■

The man would tell us stories; he'd tell us about what he used to have. Jess would respond with stories; he'd tell him what he wanted to have. Broken Chinese and fluent English, broken English and fluent Chinese: I'd watch their mouths move as they spoke words that the other didn't want to listen to. I'd watch their mouths move and I wondered if the blemishes on Jess's skin and the wrinkles on the man's face could remove themselves from their bodies and Morse code a line of dots and dashes that crossed the ocean between them.

■

He dreams for a living.

He rolls over and buries his nose in the salty smell that her hair has left on the pillow. Things would be different if this was one of his novels. He wouldn't have gone to sleep. He would have stayed up all night, pacing, biting his nails, constantly pulling back the curtains to check if she was coming down the street. He would realize that, in her hurry to pack, she had left her ring lying on the floor, the gold band shining against the stark white tiles. He would hear the bolts turn in the door and she'd be standing there in the doorway. "I left something here," she'd say. He would hold out the ring. She would say, "That's not it," and bury her head into his shoulder.

But this isn't a dream. She hadn't left in a fit of rage or because they were being mercilessly torn apart. She'd gone to Tiananmen Square to aid the protesters. He had been up eating a sallow orange when he felt the rumbling, when the faint screams and the sound of gunshots from the distance wafted through his window.

Demonstrations for democracy have no place in a romance novel. Tanks never rolled their way into his stories. And at the end of books, the girl always came back.

■

We don't talk. We'll be bringing the dishes from the kitchen to the dinner table and spooning the rice from the cooker into the bowls. Then we'll hear the loud clang of the gate closing. All three of us will stop, simultaneously look up at the clock, and know that my brother's come home by how loudly he slams the door and by the way his keys jingle when he's turning the locks. Just like how each of us knows the pattern and weight of the others' footsteps or the sounds we make while chewing over the silent dinner table. We will stop and start and bump into each other in the hallways, and our chopsticks will collide across the dinner table when we are reaching for tsai tsai. Then we will bashfully come to a halt, wait for the other to go, then both decide at the same time to go ahead ourselves and crash again.

We live in the same house. When we take showers our hairs collect in a thick mat at the drain, mine buzz-cut, my mother's permed and reddish brown, my brother's ear-length and straight, my father's the product of not changing his hairstyle since he came to America in the '70s. When our skin cells fall they cluster with everyone else's to form a fine dust on the waxed wooden boards that my mother sweeps away with her old-school straw broom. Almost everything in the house has been touched and retouched, leaving layers upon layers of each of us, our molecules clinging to the surfaces and to each other.

■

He's living for a dream.

He doesn't want to join the mob of frenzied loved ones in the hospitals. So instead he goes grocery shopping.

When he was with her he would imagine their children. He could see himself watching his son bury his round cheeks into a slice of watermelon too big for his stubby fingers to lift. He could see her smiling at the two of them as she waters tulips by the windowsill.

He carries his bags as he crosses Changan Boulevard. He stands, frozen, in the middle of it as a row of tanks rolls toward him. He wonders what can spout from the lean cannon pointing above his head.

What kind of ammunition is lined up in this machine? Can it lob watermelons, spray tulips? Can it inundate the streets of Beijing with her scent, with a father's joy?

This morning he bought enough tsai tsai to feed two adults and a small child.

■

Jess is a prick. I walk into the dining room and he and Mom are in the middle of an argument. Jess is using his rebellious anti-authority voice; Mom speaks to him in Chinese and he responds in English.

"For God's sakes, I've wanted to do this since I was five! I've spent the last, what, 11, 12 years dreaming about this, this one thing that I'm actually good at—"

"You never gave anything else the chance!" Mom gives him an exasperated, deep-throated Hei! All the while she's spooning the latest of her concoctions into our bowls. It's supposed to be green bean soup, but it looks like what you'd get if you left mashed potatoes in a dog litter. "Music major," she scoffs. "What's the use!"

I grinned. "She wants you to be a doctor. And she wants you to have grandchildren, and she wants you to live in this house forever and be a good obedient smiling bobblehead doll."

"Shut up, Ryan."

Then Mom says, "Medicine is a good field."

Jess does his neckroll-groan. I imitate him. Mom continues.

"Why not? Doctors make lots of money—"

"Is that all you care about? A job isn't always about how big the number on your paycheck is."

"Oh, snap," I say.

"Ryan, shut up."

"Your father had a medical degree before he came here. He comes, and all of a sudden it's worth nothing. So he started all over again, but he couldn't go to medical school because he had to take care of you."

For a moment, total silence. Jess licks his lips.

"You can't guilt me into this."

"Just think about it."

"I'm not changing my mind."

"Just think about it."

"I'm not changing my mind."

"You're going to college next year. After college you'll have to make your own money. What are you going to do with a music degree? Where are you going to be?"

"Onstage," he tells her. "Making music."

Mom doesn't want to respond to that. "Eat," she says, thumping the bowls onto the table.

He lives in a dream.

He touches the wooden boards with his bare feet, wiping away the sleep that had crusted in the corners of his eyes. He can stay here forever. He doesn't want to think about what has happened to her, what could have happened if he had just asked her not to go. He can stay here forever; he doesn't want to think about life or coming back down. He peels back the curtain and climbs over the ledge of the window; he steps outside and starts to run. He can smell the morning dew, crisp and sharp and green, clinging like little crystal orbs to the grass, the world still blanketed by the dark. He can stay here forever, in his dreams, running.

Jess is a prick but he's a genius. When he plays he gets lost in the steady stream of heaven that's rolling between his fingers and flooding our apartment. And we get lost with him, sometimes. My father was coming home from work one day when he stopped in the anteroom. He sat on the tiles scattered with shoes, closed his eyes and leaned the back of his head against the wall as the music seeped through the keyhole and through the crack under the door.

Jess is a prick but he's not an idiot. A few nights ago I saw him flipping through our parents' checkbook, watching the numbers plummet and rise and plummet dangerously low again. Jess is a prick but he's not an idiot. He knows how much they spend for us, how much they work for us, how much they want for us, how much they care for us, how much they love.

You can tell when Jess is about to do something stupid by the way his body winds up and stiffens like a board. He's doing it now as the old man approaches the counter with his orange.

"You can't dwell on this for the rest of your life," Jess tells him.

The man's arm is outstretched; he has the orange cupped in one brown liver-spotted hand. Jess takes it and puts it onto the counter. "I can't sell this to you."

"Thirty cents," says the old man, placing the fruit onto the scale and reading off the numbers from the green digital display.

He takes out his change. Jess pushes it back toward him. They play a bizarre game with one another, the pieces ping-ponging back and forth across the counter.

I slide from my stool. They're still at it when I return carrying a fresh orange. I bag it, take his change, and hand it to him. He peers down into the plastic bright-red depths of the bag and doesn't say a word.

■

From our room we can hear the crunching sound of something hitting the plastic garbage bags in the alley below. We ignore it at first, but the falling becomes as regular as rain. We go to our window, and we catch a glimpse of the old man before he crouches and disappears behind wall. When he resurfaces he has unidentifiable clumps between his fingers, which he releases outside of his window.

It takes us a while to realize that these are the rotting oranges he's been hoarding for the past 16 years. It takes us a while to realize that all those times when he'd come to the store, he'd bought a sallow orange that he would never eat. He'd bring it back to his bedroom, set it in its place, and surround himself with rotting fruit and the scent of a home far away.

I pull back from the window, but Jess stands there staring.

■

Eventually he moves, slowly, as if he can feel every bone in his body shifting and the fibers of his muscles sliding as he lowers himself onto the edge of his chair. He stares at his chemistry homework for a moment.

"So this ideal law of gases thing."

I look up at him, cocking an eyebrow.

"But it's not like I'm going to, um, suddenly decide to become a doctor or anything."

He plops his chemistry textbook next to mine. We hammer out the concepts and the problems together, our voices ebbing and flowing into the night.

In the moments that we fall silent, I can hear from across the alley the sound of a man who is having the tangy sweetness of an orange flood his mouth for the first time in 16 years.

SWEAT
VIVIAN TRUONG

We carry long, unwieldy bags slung over one shoulder and bouncing at the backs of our knees. Except Jenny, who carries her foil in her hands and uses a duffel bag for the rest because she's too cool for us. No one knows what to call what's in our bags. Some of us call it equipment, but that's three syllables and it's too much of a mouthful. Some of us just call it stuff. Paul calls it shit. He'll wonder out loud where his shit went, he'll ask us where our shit is, he'll yell at us to put our shit on, and when Ian tells him that he didn't bring his stuff, Paul asks, what? and Ian rolls his gray eyes and says, I didn't bring my shit. And then he understands.

We all basically carry the same equipment-stuff-shit. We carry knickers—tight white pants that reach past our knees and look good on no one—and long socks that cover up our calves. We carry white canvas or nylon jackets; most of them are soaked through before practice ends. We carry padded gloves, gray from where the foils' grips have rusted off onto the fabric. Brian never washes his and we can all smell the result. We carry lamés, the metal threads of the vest rusting green at the neck from sweat. We carry body cords that connect our blades to the scoring machines. They run under our jackets and out our sleeves, and there's a great deal of cursing and unzipping when someone forgets to put theirs on. We carry masks that are stained several shades darker than the original color. We carry bent and scratched up blades. The girls carry breast protectors, plastic cups that fit into pockets on the insides of our jackets. I lost mine last year and Jenny offered me one of hers; for a week we each fenced with one protected breast.

We all carry different shoes. Mine are covered in bright green tape ripped into shooting stars. Jenny plastered them all over for good luck; they're peeling off and the directors look at me strangely. Alex carries two pairs of shoes—one hurts and the other slides, so he wears a different shoe on each foot when he fences. Jonathan bought new fancy silver and red ones because his white old-man shoes are torn from being dragged too often on the metal strip. Max Blitzer wears Air Force One's because he likes to think he's ghetto. He wants us to call him B-Unit when we cheer but we yell A-Cup instead.

And we carry little things. Last year Jonathan wouldn't stop complaining about how we wouldn't stop jabbing near his crotch, so Jenny and I went to Modell's and bought him a jock cup for his birthday—the smallest size we could find. Brian carries alcohol wipes for his glasses; he's a computer nerd from periods one through ten, but after school he transforms like Superman and becomes our A1 and captain. I carry safety pins to hold up my secondhand knickers passed down from Grace, captain from two years ago who cared about the little freshmen.

Last year Jenny, Brian, Paul, and I carried laminated nametags clipped to our dress shirts. We were accepting a donation to the team at the Yale Club and spent the time figuring out how to spell hors d'oeuvres. It was the first time in my life I've ever eaten an artichoke, an artichoke with cheese around it, breaded and fried and put on a silver platter covered in lacy cloth. We sat in the back being obnoxious high school kids. Once in a while the speakers would say something and there would be a murmur of chuckles. I would squint at Paul and he would say, It's sophisticated humor, Vivian, now laugh with me. Ohohohoho. When we were released we sat down at a diner, making fun of ourselves and the others on the team and the people at the Yale Club, cracking up with ham and swiss clenched between our teeth.

We carry music. When we go to playoffs we take a cheese bus to the Bronx and someone carries a boom box with a CD full of war music. There's "We Will Rock You." Last year Matt, the six-foot redhead, sang the bridges—You got mud on your face/You big disgrace/

Somebody better put you back into your place—and the rest of us sang the chorus, stomping our feet on the bus floor and clapping to the rhythm: boom-boom-chk, boom-boom-chk, we will, we will, rock you. There's "Can't Touch This," which of course is the theme song for us Untouchables. Two years ago, Grace made us all learn the words to "Eye of the Tiger." We'd save it until the bus was about to pull up to the gym and we'd sing it so loudly that we couldn't hear our own individual voices over everyone else's. Then we'd flood out of the bus, bags over our shoulders, ready to plow the other teams over.

We carry defiance against the splitting of the co-ed team last year. We sneak into each others' practices. We egg each other on in matches. When one of our teammates screams after scoring a touch, we scream with them. I scream ahp, Jonathan yells bao, Brian says hoopah, and Ian shouts baaAAaaAAh. We scream and clap and yell nicknames until we have sore throats and red palms. While the opposing team is yelling John or Mary, we're yelling Mattmobile and A-Cup.

We carry our losses. Like last year's semifinals match against Hunter; we'd dive-bombed from first to fourth in one year. One of the Hunter moms offered us homemade oatmeal raisin cookies. We stared at them. I'm allergic to oats.

We carry tears. There's no teammate to hide behind on the strip, just you and the fencer at the other end. Each touch scored on you can hurt, and humiliate, and each time the blade slips past your defenses and you hear the machine beep your opponent's touch, your heart drops a little. After Megan was eliminated from a tournament that we both know she could've won, we stood leaning with our backs against the walls on opposite sides of an empty bathroom and we started name-calling the girl she couldn't beat. It got so stupid that she started to garble out a laugh; she nodded when I told her there's always a next time to come back and kick butt.

We carry, not just wins, but victories. Like the girls' match against Hunter, the break in our school's four-game losing streak against them.

Like Brian's bout against their A1, the big-shot Junior Olympics first-place winner. Like the tiebreaker of the tiebreaker of the tiebreaker against Tottenville. Like the finals two years ago against Bronx Science, which had pushed us down to silver in the year before. Grace bought a box of Entenmann's mini chocolate chip cookies from the Hole in the Wall and held it up on the bus. You see these? she asked us. We're not eating them unless we win. We watched David fence the deciding bout in total silence. There were ticks of metal hitting metal. Attack. Parry. Disengage. Riposte. The scoring machine rang. And we exploded. And the cookies were so, so sweet.

We carry pieces of each other. Not just breast protectors and other equipment-stuff-shit. We carry inside jokes, we carry crushes on one another, we carry each others' skin cells from all the clappings-on-the-back. We carry the burning lactic acid in our legs that we all endure together when we do conditioning—if there are 20 other people who are feeling the same thing it doesn't hurt nearly as much. When we make huddles before and after meets, we are a mass of wet armpits and everyone is carrying everyone else's sweat and it's disgusting but it's love. We pile our hands on top of one another's and we all scream Touch this! because damn, we're strong together.

STARGAZING
VICTORIA COLE, 17
SOUTH CAROLINA GOVERNOR'S SCHOOL FOR THE ARTS
AND HUMANITIES
GREENVILLE, SC
TEACHERS: ASHLEY WARLICK, MAMIE MORGAN

"Somewhere, something incredible is waiting to be known."
—Carl Sagan

It's 9 a.m., a Saturday morning, and my mother would like to do
some laundry. When she comes through the kitchen, however, and into
the laundry room, the washing machine is full, though there are no
clothes inside. Instead, there is me, curled carefully inside the washer,
my seven- or eight-year-old body fitting easily inside. Over the glass
window I have taped a picture of outer space cut from a magazine. The
clipping is curling up at the edges.

Earth, a swirl of ocean and land, of heartbreak and miracle invisible from such heights, hovers far away, in the bright space I am pretending to inhabit. Within the washer, I expand this damp, dark
corner into bright, sharp-edged outer space, where I am no one—it
is only me, floating in this emptiness, and perhaps I, too, am ethereal, as planets might be imagined, or stars, bits of crushed ice, dust,
gas. Perhaps I, too, have no substance. But simultaneously, I am
someone—the only solid thing for thousands of miles, a whole universe of insubstantiality—fields of ghostly stars and asteroids, broken pieces of worlds, light spiraling out into nothingness, but still
I exist, boldly whole. Only I exist. Here, gravity means nothing.
Less than nothing—less than, at this age, love, cleanliness, the art
of good manners.

My mother, her hands full of soiled shirts, rags, and undergarments, kicks lamely at the window of the washer. "What are you doing in there?" she asks.

"Nothing," I say.

"Hurry up. My hands are full." Her voice is thin with impatience. I press my hands against the glass and kick, rolling my way out of the rubbery lips of the washing machine to escape back into the sunny glare, the electricity of the summer afternoon. After my disappearance, my mother simply crouches in front of the machine to fill it with clothing. When I returned to the laundry room, the magazine clipping had been peeled from the glass.

We never mention the incident again, but still I wonder what my mother thought, finding me in the recesses of the washer. Did she think me a strange child, maladjusted, that this was another of my strange ideas? Or was she even a little proud of my interest in space—pleased by my apparent interest in the sciences, a field that, in her eyes, granted me a promising future? If it was the latter, she would, in time, be sorely disappointed. My mother liked books, but saw no future in writing them. Pursuing such a career was naïve and impractical when other, more sensible paths could be chosen—a doctor, an engineer, or at the very least, a lawyer. During those years, however, my mother's wishes were temporarily granted in a small way: I wanted to be an astronaut.

I wanted both the anonymity and eminence that outer space promised. I wanted the blackness, the sharp pinpoints of light that, even from a spaceship, were too far away to comprehend. Besides, I almost wanted to preserve their distance, their smallness and delicateness, as they were. Transformed, they would be unconquerably large.

I always find it strange that while space became a long-term obsession, the rest of the world—or at least the Western Hemisphere—became disturbingly uninterested in space. In the late '90s, people everywhere tried to reinvent space, to rekindle a dying interest. There were new television series about space, new space missions planned to Mars and Saturn, and new planetarium programs. Nothing worked. As

Nicholas Wapshott wrote in the *London Times*, "Ask a seven-year-old boy what he wants to be when he grows up and 'an astronaut' will not be on the list." No one else shared my dream. The space obsession haunting the past four decades as a result of the space race had disappeared: in the '90s, space was out. Public interest could not be revived. As alleged in a 1997 article on Mars, curiosity about space had been lost for the first time since the discovery of the universe. As early as the 1600s, astronomers such as Galileo, Kepler, and Huygens began telescopically monitoring space, studying it intensely. Since then, it had been a subject of great public interest. In the 20th century, people watched with great enthusiasm the take-offs of ships speeding into oblivion, have seen in their television sets the Earth itself, insignificant in cold, airless space. The foreign nature of the emptiness intrigued the masses. As Fred Langa of *Byte* magazine reminds us, "At the dawn of the era of artificial satellites, it was not unusual to see neighbors clustered on darkened street corners, necks bent upward, trying to catch a glimpse of some newly launched Sputnik or Explorer or Echo."

Somewhere in the late stages of elementary school, my class embarks on a trip to the city planetarium. From the outside, it doesn't look like much: a square, dark-bricked building with a cracked parking lot where the bus drops us off. Inside, there are four or five rows of seats, all on one level, and in the middle of the dome squats a giant projector, already lit up and ready to go, though the lights are still on. Soon, when we settle down and the noise level is down to a loud whispering, a woman stands near the projector, ready to talk to us. After her primary chatter about the majesty of the stars, she settles in to talk about the myths of the constellations. While she describes each, I have trouble seeing the pictures in the stars. None of them seem to form patterns.

"Andromeda was a princess in Greece. Her father gave her to a sea monster who wanted to eat her, but Perseus saved her in the nick of time.

He decided to be her husband. Then, the Greek gods put pictures of them up in the sky as a representation of their bravery." She indicates the connect-the-dots picture of Andromeda in the "sky" above us. Many of my peers seem confused by this explanation. I myself do not understand why Andromeda's bravery was celebrated, considering that she did nothing to stop the sea monster from eating her. I raise my hand, waving it frantically in front of the projector in order to be seen in the darkness.

"Yes?"

"So if we do something brave, will we get put up in the stars? By the Greek people?" I am thrilled at the prospect of seeing a picture of myself in the sky, no matter how hard it is to connect the dots. She looks embarrassed, and clears her throat.

"No. Only . . . " this woman seems put off by my question. "Only famous people get put in the sky," she says. "Not regular people." I tell her I do not think that is fair.

"Well, that's the way things are," she says, and continues her lecture on to Canus Major.

As upset as I am by the favoritism displayed by the Greek people who put pictures in the sky, whom I would not learn more about until middle school, I decide I can deal with that. Perhaps, I think, if I grow up to be an astronaut and discover a new planet, as I often imagine doing, I, too, could be considered famous enough to be made into a constellation. This became my goal for the next several years. I became obsessed with the idea of heading into space—of seeing the crystallized rings of Saturn, the craters of the moon, the impact of an asteroid—for myself.

No one quite agrees on the reason for the recently evolved disinterest in outer space. Langa concurs with popular belief: there hasn't been much interest in space since the Cold War because of a lack of motivation. There are no Russians to race to the finish, and there is no moon to dream of. It has become a reality, no longer a hope or a promise but cold, hard fact: been there, done that. The things that we have not seen already are unreachable. We can launch a mission to Mars, but people cannot journey there. This does not interest us. As for other places—even more distant places, which we cannot see even in our telescopes—those are rendered that much more impossible by our limited technology. We can't even dream of venturing to these places that we cannot see a glimmer of. The otherworldliness of this suggestion is relegated to movies, to fiction. Reality cannot encompass such dreams.

But others find different reasons. Wapshott dismisses the newly budding space station, blaming it for the recent disinterest. People aren't interested in a space station built for observation. What matters to the American people is forward motion—the escape to another world, another galaxy. And, more importantly, the search for extraterrestrial life.

Which leads us to another reason interest in space might be waning: a lack of interest in the kind of "life" that may or may not be out there. Before Kennedy's mission to put man on the moon, people thought of extraterrestrial life as sentient. Green men? Huge robots? They could be anywhere. If we exist, why can't every planet be so lucky to be populated too? The voice of reason had not yet been established, and people expected that if other life existed, it would be big. With recent observations, however, it has become evident that if life does exist elsewhere, it probably isn't much more than bacteria. This is not the stuff of fantasy—worlds the size of toothbrush bristles do not count, in the public's eye, as extraterrestrial life.

As time passed, I began to realize that an astronaut, perhaps, was not the best profession for me. I excelled at reading and writing at school, did well in English and history courses, but was a disaster at algebra. Nor did I enjoy earth science or chemistry. To be an engineer, a pilot, or for that matter, anything useful aboard a spaceship, I would have to be proficient in these fields. I found I enjoyed writing more than any of these things, and enrolled in an arts and humanities-based magnet in high school instead of applying for the science and math magnet at the rival school. Both my parents and my desire to be an astronaut seemed to counteract my talents, the inner workings of my brain. Periodically, I fretted about this.

One of these times was on a trip to Disney World on the eve of my youngest brother's seventh birthday. We stood in line, waiting to get on Space Mountain, and the building that housed it was full of space paraphernalia. The walls were covered with screens displaying asteroids, Saturn, Venus, and Jupiter flying through space. I quickly became transfixed by the possibilities they embodied, was reminded of a trip to space camp years before, when I was given the role of a pilot during the simulation. I remembered the pride I felt, even though I knew it wasn't real. It was still where I belonged. I felt a sudden burst of melancholy.

"I wish I could still be an astronaut."

My father did not turn from the space-covered walls when I spoke. "You can still be one if you major in a science field in college," he answered, unperturbed. On other occasions he seemed more engaged in my future, but now seemed tired of hearing my worries voiced.

"But I like writing, not science," I said, biting my lip. My father shrugged.

"Write grants for NASA." This idea had not occurred to me, but it still did not seem a feasible one. Always on the sidelines, I would have no chance to go into space. I decided I could think about this later. I would find a way to be an astronaut, if that was still what I wanted.

"Do you think it's stupid to still want to be an astronaut in high school?"

My father did not answer. I turned back to the starry walls to watch an asteroid career through space.

■

There are other possibilities for the current disinterest in space. One reason often cited is that the reality of space exploration becomes uninteresting beside the romanticized, fictionalized accounts Hollywood has provided in the movies, an idea Langa finds comical because of the irony: all of Hollywood's space films depend on technology that is largely the result of the space program's findings. It can be said, however, that much of what we have not yet discovered can be found on the TV screen: planets we cannot dream of traveling to have been colonized in the movies. It is true that we may be more interested in these dreams than the reality we cannot yet reach, may never be able to reach. Perhaps we will never achieve the kind of technology needed to move beyond the Milky Way—the kind of technology people see in the movies.

Perhaps the most interesting reason cited for a deflation of interest in outer space is a very different idea: that the sight of Earth from space scared the American public. Paul Hoffman of *Discover* magazine says, "From the vantage point of space it was clear that Earth's atmosphere was a thin shell, like the skin of an onion, and not a boundless layer that could suffer whatever abuse—whatever pollutants—we foisted on it." Rumors of global warming and air pollution became cold, hard fear. We discovered how small we are, how fleeting our planet could be. Buzz Aldrin himself observed that the Earth looked so small, he could erase it from the universe with only his thumb. According to some, it is this viewpoint that drove Americans from space. They did not want to be reminded of the damage they were causing every day. The vulnerability of our planet was much too frightening; it was better for them not to see such things, but to simply go about their days thinning out our atmosphere spared the guilt they might have felt otherwise. Better to glance upwards and see a reassuringly opaque blue sky. Better not to see our thin shell.

■

The night was strangely warm for Cedar Mountain. Usually, the days were unbearably hot, and the nights were chilly enough to require a sweatshirt, enough to make you want to huddle together, to collapse your arms inside your shirt to stop goose bumps from forming. Tonight, though, we wandered from our cabins in shorts and bare feet, feeling summer, with the grass alive beneath our toes. Our counselor led us to the dock, where we curled on yoga mats to watch the sky. The wood felt young and splintery; the dock had just been built the previous spring. The sky is distantly black, full of stars—bare in the way the sky can only be in the mountains, hidden from the city lights. Simple silver splotches on the emptiness of black, unmarred by fog, clouds, light pollution. A silver dollar moon hung in the middle.

A sudden streak of orange exploded in the corner of my eye—a fire-fly, I thought briefly, but no—a shooting star, like a rocket, shot across the sky. It seemed four-dimensional, perhaps, speeding not only through space, but through time, shooting through hours like sheets of glass, changing the course of history in a burst of starshine. It was my first shooting star, and I was 12 years old. Gasps erupted around me as the other girls spotted the same phenomenon. My counselor, Erin, had a con-flicted look on her face; one of joy, and of fear. I did not understand this.

I thought about where the star might have landed. I wondered what they are made of, once they strike the atmosphere. Did they land whole, five-pointed, like sizzling starfish? I guess I must have known that wasn't true, but still, I assumed a shooting star was just that: a star. I later learned that they have nothing to do with stars; they are simply meteoroids burning up as they fall through Earth's atmosphere. If a broken piece survives, it crashes somewhere, becoming slag, a melted rock from space. Despite the romanticism of the fictionalized "falling star," the meteorite is, perhaps, even more amazing—a piece of a bro-ken world, a fractured life, falling to Earth.

THE LEFT AND THE LEAVING
VICTORIA COLE

At the end of sophomore year, there is a routine drug search. The searches are supposed to be randomly conducted, but our classroom doesn't get searched because we're in advanced classes. They don't search advanced classes. We're in the CavPlex room, which means that instead of walls we have windows, so we can see the drug search being conducted in the hallway. Wash, my AP European History teacher, is getting frustrated because she can tell we aren't paying attention to her lesson. It's a stunt we wouldn't usually pull, because Wash, in spite of looking like someone's grandmother, is a very imposing person. Her short stature and slight potbelly are negated by her imperious manner, and her face is much like an eagle's. She is in charge of just about everything at the school, and she rules with an iron fist. The events outside, however, are interesting enough for us to risk her wrath.

In the hallway, my friend Jackson is in a line of students. He looks nervous. A policeman brings a German shepherd down the line, and he sniffs each kid. All the kids in the hallway look bewildered as the dog sniffs each one; this is just a dog, like every other dog they have encountered. It is hard to see this dog as a drug detector, as something that has the potential to ruin lives. It is only a dog. But the dog sniffs anyways, searching. Sometimes he stops at someone, and they search them, right there in the hallway. It seems like it should be a more intimate act, something to conduct in private. They don't find anything; none of them are holding. So the dog moves on. He doesn't seem to sense that what he finds can land someone in a bad place. He stops at Jackson, and barks once.

Everyone knows Jackson. He's been in and out of a relationship with my best friend, Kate, since fifth grade, even though he asked me out four times in sixth. We've all been in school together as long as we can remember; he sat next to me in sixth grade English and entertained me with stories about his escapades with his older brother, egging cars and other things smart kids aren't supposed to do. So he forfeited his position, and moved into regular classes. He didn't follow us into magnet programs and advanced classes. This year, he is repeating freshman year, and although he never quite fit in, he is still one of us. Everyone holds their breath when the German shepherd pushes his nose closer to Jackson, intrigued by something he smells. Jackson's eyes go wide and he backs against the wall, cornered. The policeman smiles grimly, like a prison guard. The dog leans closer, but before he can bark, Jackson bolts. He's down the hall within seconds, with the police officer yelling after him. His shoes squeak against the linoleum. The officer runs after him. At this point, our class's rapt attention to the situation is broken.

"This is a class, you know!" Wash says shrilly, slamming a book down onto Stephen's desk. Stephen happened to have been staring open-mouthed out the window. We all jump, and turn around to pay attention, or at least act like we are. For the rest of the lesson, Wash tries to pretend nothing happened, but her jaw is clenched tighter than usual. The moment of Jackson's flight repeats itself over and over in my head; I see his shoe twisting as he turns to run, and his scared blue eyes.

■

It is Thanksgiving, and we have all piled our plates full of the food that everyone brought—Aunt Susan always makes mac and cheese, and Aunt Karen always makes three bean salad. Aunt Julie never made the same thing twice; last year, it was fairy pudding. I still remember the light, fluffy feel of the pudding on my tongue, and the graham cracker dust caking inside my mouth.

"I got the recipe from our relatives in Idaho," Julie said.

I licked my spoon. "I want to go to Idaho," I said.

"You can come with us sometime," she said. "Maybe next year. It's pretty out there."

That year, it was almost warm on Thanksgiving and all the kids went out by the creek while Julie and my mother sat inside and hummed James Taylor—Goodnight, you moonlight ladies, rock-a-bye sweet baby James. When I came back inside, Carl got out his guitar and sang for us, and Julie's smile couldn't have stretched wider. She loved it when he sang.

This year, her chair is empty. Uncle Carl looks pale and drawn; it has only been three days since she died. Everyone is treating him like he might do something desperate, but he looks like he doesn't have the energy. I doubt he's slept in the past couple of days. My cousins are sitting beside him; Andrew says nothing, and Chris is talking loud and fast enough to make up for it. It is clear that Chris shaved this morning, but Andrew has not, and I see that his fingernails are long and ragged when he picks up his fork. It will stay this way for a long time, and people will whisper behind their packs about the way grief can manifest itself for years. I cannot blame either of them for their reactions, and I can't say either was more destroyed by it than the other. Chris laughs at Aunt Karen's half-hearted joke, but his voice is trembling. Andrew leaves before dinner starts. It will be two years until he shows up at another family dinner.

Thanksgiving is relentless, and has come despite our troubles, and so we are eating, but not with our natural gusto. I almost resent the holiday for coming on time. Everyone seems to be looking at her empty seat. It is hard to ignore the fact that someone who should be sitting at the table is simply not there. The only person who does not glance at the empty chair, however briefly, is Andrew. He looks down at his plate, mostly. The turkey my mother made this year is too dry, and everyone has to douse it with gravy. Its dryness surprises me; my mother has always been a good cook. When we clear the table, the white linen tablecloth is soiled with spots of gravy, cranberries from my mother's stuffing, and candied yams, because everyone put too much food on their plate, like everyone does on Thanksgiving. The difference is, nobody eats all of their food this year. I don't even get seconds. My dad only eats one slice of pumpkin pie. Pumpkin pie is his favorite. Everyone stops trying to act like everything is okay when there is a turkey leg left uneaten, and it is dead quiet while my mother and I clear the table. At Julie's spot, the linen is still the same perfect white it was when we sat down to eat.

■

I drive Jackson home one day, a week before the school formally expels him for possession of marijuana. It is a strange period of time— we know that he leaves soon, but he is still at school now. We don't say much for the first mile or so.

"If I were you," I say, "I'd just not come to school. You know they're going to kick you out anyway."

"Yeah," he says. "I might as well stay." This is not a statement with which I can argue, so we don't say much for a mile or so. I take a left at a stoplight. "Oh, actually you need to take a right," he says.

"No, Longbrook is this way. I know how to get to your house, stupid," I say.

He seems more serious than usual. "No," he says. "I don't live there anymore."

"Oh," I say. It seems there is nothing to say to this. I turn around in a driveway and he gives me some directions. I notice that his hands are clenched stiff in his lap; it is cold outside and they are also red and chapped, raw from the wind.

"Where did you guys move?" I ask, innocently enough. He doesn't answer for a while.

"Quail Run," he says finally. I don't say anything to that—what can I say? Quail Run is a run-down apartment complex a few miles away from the neighborhood I live in—where Jackson used to live. "My dad kicked us out," he says eventually. In this moment, he seems vulnerable.

"I'm sorry," I say. We pull into Quail Run. There is a woman hanging up her laundry on a balcony to the left of the gate. He mumbles something about his dad being a dick. I ask him which way his apartment is, left or right.

"Right," he says, "All the way down. My mom doesn't have a job. I was going to have to drop out anyways, I guess." This seems to be the heart of his anxiety.

"What about Spencer?" I ask. Spencer is Jackson's brother. I figure he must live there, too; he hasn't done anything since he dropped out of college.

"With my dad," he says. I don't know what to say to this, either, but we've reached his apartment so it doesn't matter. I reach to put the car into park and Jackson grasps my hand briefly, quickly squeezing it and then releasing. I look over and he smiles half-heartedly as he unbuckles his seat belt.

"Well," I tell him, "At least now you had to leave. Now you won't be always thinking that you shouldn't have dropped out, because you didn't have a choice." He laughs a little and admits that it's true. I have never been very good at cheering people up. Jackson opens the door and steps out of the car.

"Thanks for the ride," he says. "Guess I'll see you around." He touches my shoulder and half-smiles, then shuts the door. I watch him go up and unlock the apartment, and then head home. Jackson doesn't show up to class the next day. Nobody sees him at school ever again after that. I saw him at a couple of parties, but he moved to Charleston a few months after. School got quieter. There was no one to dip and spit at lunch or throw food at the freshmen, or pick up girls and twirl them around until they screamed with laughter. Even in the year to come, when I end up at a school where I don't know anyone, I still notice his absence.

Thanksgiving was also the last time I saw my Uncle John. It was the Thanksgiving before Julie died, which is always hard for me to remember, because the two time spans have become so muddled in my head. He was my mother's brother, and the whole family called him J.R. He remembered the phone numbers of every house he had ever lived in since the age of three and he drank too much. On Thanksgiving, John was drunk, but he wasn't angry, as he often was. After everyone else had helped clean up and gone home, my parents and I sat with John out on the patio, watching the fire. We were running out of wood fast. My dad made a joke about going into the backyard to cut down a tree.

"Danny," my mother protested, but he and John just laughed. There were no logs left, only some long pieces of lumber my dad had left over from the tree house he'd built for my little brother. John picked up some of the lumber and set one piece on top of the other.

"I used to be pretty good at this in karate," he said, and kicked the piece of lumber with some force. Immediately he grabbed his foot, cursing and yelling that he thought he'd broken his toe. Within a minute, though, he had forgotten all about it and we were all laughing. My dad and John eventually got the wood broken into manageable pieces without breaking any bones and we burned it.

"I hope there aren't any fumes or anything," my mother said, biting her lip. I decided not to tell her that the lumber probably did have chemicals in it, having been treated. "Another One Bites the Dust" came on the stereo my dad had installed on the patio.

"We used to love this song," my mom said to John with a wistful smile. "And another one bites the dust," she sang along, out of tune. My mother has never been much of a singer.

"One of the few songs we both liked," John said with a snort.

"I don't know about that," she said, her voice mild, resonating against the walls because the music had stopped playing.

"You liked a bunch of terrible music. I can remember going into my closet so I couldn't hear your…Helen Reddy, that was what it was. God-awful," he said.

My mother mock-gasped. "You just can't appreciate Helen for what she is," she said, laughing. "You're nothing but a sexist!"

John laughed. "Yeah, well Helen Reddy is a dyke!" My mother laughed in spite of herself, and John stood up in front of the fire, and he sang "I Am Woman" for everyone. His voice was slurred a little bit, and my mother was laughing harder than I'd seen her laugh in a long time. Soon after he finished his rendition of "I Am Woman," we all headed for bed. It was around two, which was the latest I'd ever known my parents to stay up. John stayed in the office on the pull-out couch, and didn't wake up until four the next afternoon.

About a month and a half after that Thanksgiving, John got into a car wreck in the mountains, in Wyoming. We had the funeral in South Carolina, though, and my mother was so upset that she forgot me at the church when they left for the gravesite. I had to walk the two miles back to my house.

My friends and I walked down the sidewalk on our way home from the grocery store, and happen to pass a cemetery. Before we pass it, we talk and laugh freely.

"We are so far from our home," Jasmine says in a sing-song voice, and we laugh because it is only a mile back to school. Then we fall silent; there is a sudden feeling of solemnity, a certain gravity in the air. At first, I don't know the source, but decide to obey the feeling in the back of my throat anyhow, to bend to its will and join in the silence. It isn't until we look toward the cemetery that we notice the burial in process. The family is standing to one side of the coffin. Most of their faces are wet with tears, and they bend over, some of them crumpled with grief. There is one boy in particular who catches my eye; he has a goatee and wears black jeans; he looks about 20 and more angry than sad. His arms are folded tightly over his chest and he stares at something far away. I feel almost certain that his mother has died. I have seen that look before on many faces—cousins, mostly, people I've known all my life, but there is no other kind of grief that looks this way. There is a certain set to the jaw, a sorrow that carries anger more visibly than other deaths. When we get close, I see that the boy's jaw is trembling. His legs look too thin in his black jeans. I watch him until we walk past the cemetery, until he is no longer visible. He doesn't seem to notice. He is the source of the solemnity in the air, the heavy sadness pressing down on my head. My friends and I say nothing until we are well past the cemetery's gates. Eventually, we slip back into conversation, and we don't talk about the burial again. Still, I can't forget the look on the boy's face, and it makes me think about absences, and how they affect people. Grief is about loss; it comes with death and distance. There are other smaller things, though, that can produce a similar grief. I feel much the same when absence occurs in minute ways, such as finishing a load of laundry and finding only one sock out of the pair, or going out on a cold night and seeing no stars because of the cloudy skies. It is the absence of something that creates the feeling: when someone who should be eating dinner isn't there, when a piece of jewelry you always wear leaves an empty strip of skin. I wonder what the last words the boy with the black jeans said to his mother were, even though I don't know that it his mother who died. On the walk back, I think about rooms without windows.

It is late afternoon on Thanksgiving, and we have just finished eating our holiday dinner. Everyone is napping except for my cousin Matt and me. We venture out of the cabin and down the dirt road to sit by the heart-shaped lake. We sit down in the snow and I can immediately feel the snow seeping through my jeans. Matt passes me a cigarette and I accept it. It has been a hard week. Every time I think about John I can't help but feel envy, because these people, his wife's family, were the ones he spent his last years with. We were his real family, the one he was born into. It doesn't seem fair that they were the ones he spent his time with, hundreds of miles away from South Carolina.

"What are you thinking about?" Matt asks me. He is one of those people who always wants to know what's going on in your head.

"John," I say. The lake has dried up for winter and its emptiness is disconcerting. Under the snow I can see the cracks in the mud.

"It's hard for everyone," Matt says. "Especially at this time of year." I try to consider this. It has been three years since he died. I think about how everyone reacted when we got off the plane. Aunt Laurie said we all look like him. "It's like seeing him again, it takes your breath away at first," she said. After she said that I looked at myself in the mirror for a long time. I didn't see it, but all the Randolphs said they did.

"It just seems like maybe he's still really far away to me, in Wyoming or something, and he's coming to visit on Christmas," I say.

"We aren't far from Wyoming," Matt says.

"Usually I am," I say, and stare into what was once the lake.

"Yeah," Matt says. He is silent for a long time. "The lake will fill up again. Whenever spring comes all the ice melts and the glaciers move and it all pours into every crack and gap you can see." He stretches his arms wide to encompass the entire mountain range.

"I'd like to see that," I say, and we get up to head back to the cabin.

SELECTIONS FROM GOLD & SILVER AWARDS

STUDENTS IN GRADES 7–12 SUBMIT WORK IN ELEVEN WRITING CATEGORIES. THIS YEAR, MORE THAN 20,000 WRITING SUBMISSIONS WERE REVIEWED BY AUTHORS, EDUCATORS, AND LITERARY PROFESSIONALS. GOLD AND SILVER AWARDS WERE BESTOWED TO WORKS THAT DEMONSTRATED ORIGINALITY, TECHNICAL SKILL AND EMERGENCE OF A PERSONAL VOICE.

TOURIST
AMELIA WOLF, 16
ST. MARY'S ACADEMY
PORTLAND, OR
TEACHER: SARA SALVI

The stray cats in Jerusalem always seem to be smaller. Not just skinnier, but more diminutive, as if the nearness of the sun causes them to shrink into themselves. In a city where the hills rise closer to the sky and stones make you squint and you can smell fresh bread and pita from every corner, hidden things, poor things, remain hidden. In a city that spreads from the oldest center; in a city with Jews, Muslims, Armenians and Christians; in a city with Greek neighborhoods and German colonies, in a city keeping Ethiopians and Russians in the corners, room for strays diminishes with every birth and every immigrant. Only small ones appear—small ones and their mothers on the walls, mothers in the garbage, mothers everywhere but Ben Yehuda with the tourists. The stray cats don't show up near the tourists but prefer the dirtiest streets with the garbage piles. Jerusalem is golden; Jerusalem is holy. Poverty has no place in Jerusalem.

My father, who had decades ago tied himself to Israel, and now finds that tie fraying with politics and distance, insists that he isn't a tourist. This confuses me because he doesn't live here, but he explains that he used to, and he speaks Hebrew, and he isn't lost. I don't point out that my accent sounds more sabra than his, better than his, and that he is lost. I don't point out that he speaks like an American, without the guttural sounds that match the earth here. But the city believes him and dirty streets, along with stray cats and beggars, find us. Here, sweat and spices wrinkle my nose, here the people are Jews like us—because everybody is Jewish like us—but here is Arabic and hummus, and sesame-tachina. Here my father shows me the best falafel. Here, the skin isn't European and the hair is thicker. Here, there are lots of cats: small cats, skinny cats, complaining cats.

When my father thinks of tourism, he sees himself in a straw hat and a Hawaiian T-shirt. A chunky camera around his neck. Tourism twists Hebrew into shouted English and arrogance. Tourists buy cheap and expensive Judaica from the King David Hotel and frequent the Roman ruins from thousands of years back. Tourists stay in the Holy Land. They never see the cafés in Tel Aviv or the ports in Haifa. So, no, of course he's not a tourist. He sees the Israel of the present and of the secular '70s. We breathe the European infused air and culture and live in the New City, not the Old. West Jerusalem is built with stones, yes, but the streets are paved with tar. The cars honk. The donkeys of the Old City do not.

We still aren't tourists when we return to the German Colony, because in the courtyard of the old, tiled Arabic house, I see a stray cat. A kitten, a tiny kitten that mews in a pitch too high for my father to hear. All I can see is a ball of fur and bones with glittering eyes that gives me a picture I can put alongside the word "pitiful." It shrinks against the glorified Jerusalem stone, even though the fruit trees crowd over the enclosure.

"Where's its mother?" we ask, my sister and I.

"She may have died," our mother replied. She must be right, because a mother never abandons her children.

"Is he going to die too?" I ask. Gavriella just turned seven and she shouldn't think about dying kittens. And I don't want to know the answer.

"Don't name it," our mother answers.

I go up to the room I've borrowed from the girl who usually lives here and stare up at the Arabic house with the high tiled ceiling. I start praying in Hebrew. The only prayers I have memorized are generic prayers that have nothing to do with kittens.

For the next week, my mother crumbles crackers in organic milk. My father takes the bus downtown and takes refresher Talmud courses in

Hebrew and English. I can imagine living here. I do live here. For the first time, I understand kneeling by the waters of Babylon, crying and harping for Zion, even if no one had been there. The dry air stings with longing, and the language starts to sound like the land: guttural, with all the sounds emanating from deep in the throat. It's too hot for the front of the mouth, for dunes south of the city. I swallow my consonants, and it can be hard to separate words. It's hard to separate the land too; the region resists borders. I think that maybe the Middle East is so angry because the languages are so fluid, and the people are so tactile. It's not a place for confinement and definition. Middle Easterners know that. Semites resist partitioning.

When we return from walks and gelato, my mother has set out chipped ceramic dishes with blue flower patterns filled with bits of soggy cracker soaking in milk in the shaded courtyard. The kitten begins to know her, and she sometimes dips dishtowels in the bowl and lets the kitten lick and suck at the milk. Each day in the afternoon, my sister and I bring back fresh lychee fruit to the apartment and we get an update on the kitten.

I start to spend more time in the courtyard. Walking into the gated garden outside the old Arab building is like arriving in Oz from Kansas, except that instead of an absence of color on the outside I can feel an absence of breeze. The Jerusalem sun, living much closer than the Portland one, denies shade, and the shadow provided by the walls and fruit trees on the inside grant a sort of sanctuary. The courtyard is an overgrown Alhambra, with its citrus smells and sounds of rushing water. I imagine it a harem garden, contrasting with the common and choking heat outside the gates.

Israelies have a much smaller sense of personal space, and I, the Portlander who remembers privacy, am safe here from the jostling and the shouting and the "What is your problem, can't you see she was first in line, for god's sake!" Inside the courtyard, the car horns sound much farther away, muffled by the dilapidated blue and white mossy tiles.

Each afternoon when we return with the lychee fruit, my mother frowns. The kitten doesn't gain weight; it doesn't grow. But each day, I think of names, though none fit. That ends up being for the best because, according to Mom, names breed attachment. One day when we come back to the apartment, our mother shakes her head. I go up into my room and cry onto the bedspread, and glare at the old right-wing bumper stickers covering the bookshelves. I wish it were my room, not a rented one, so that I could grieve in peace. When I leave the room, the pillows are wet.

My sister, mother and I convene at the kitchen island and eat the lychee fruit, I think they taste too sweet, but there is something so exotic, so Mediterranean, about their prickly outsides and green, juicy insides that makes me claim I love them. When I eat them, I feel more Israeli, and I can close my eyes and picture myself understanding every word of the Pokémon television show dubbed into Hebrew that my sister and I watch most mornings. When I eat the lychees, I am less of a tourist.

Later that night, our family takes a walk toward the Old City. Gavriella and I skip ahead of our parents. I start speaking to her in Hebrew, and she insists in answering in English. "Amelia, I don't want to speak Hebrew anymore; why can't we just speak English?" and before I can argue, she runs farther ahead of me, toward the play-structure and park. I glare after her and feel irrationally angry, as if she is the reason that I am not Israeli. Usually, I'd follow her, but I hang back until my parents catch up. When they do, my father will speak Hebrew with me.

I will realize how hard it is to be tourists in a land that we feel so connected to, a land that we somehow think of as home because two thousand years ago we lived here. At home we still cling to just in case, after centuries of wandering and expulsions. In the back of our minds, even in America, we prepare for pogroms and libels. But Israel is a land of paratroopers and tough calluses, ready to take us in with our own right of return. Later, back in Portland where animals are large in the wet, cold air, I am homesick.

THE CHURCH OF GOD WITH SIGNS FOR FOLLOWERS WITHOUT DWELLINGS

WYNNE HUNGERFORD, 15

FINE ARTS CENTER
GREENVILLE, SC
TEACHER: CLAIRE BATEMAN

An alligator swallowed the cross
in front of the church
during fellowship one Wednesday.
Children playing by the water's edge
climbed mossy cypresses
to hide from the snapping jaws.

Commotion on the bayou
caused the service to end in uproar.
As the handlers loosened their grips,
gold-patterned snakes escaped,
coiling beneath pews
and settling like ribbons
into the creases of hymnals.
The reverend tried to appease the congregation
by hurling a Bible out the window
to scare away the beast, but it only served
as an appetizer.

Shreds of gold paper remained uneaten,
floating like blossoms across the water.
The alligator slipped into the smooth, black swamp,
to return periodically
for God's aftertaste.

THE DREAMBOOK FOR INCONSEQUENTIAL LIVES

ALICE RHEE, 17

NORTHERN VALLEY REGIONAL HIGH SCHOOL AT DEMAREST
DEMAREST, NJ
TEACHER: MARISA JANUZZI

I. Unique Baby Names

You stand behind the cash register at Heavenly Hotdogs, thinking ludicrous thoughts. You smile because Kiley was forced to man the deep fryer today, which you hate for the bubbling burns it lashes at you, and because Kiley is a bitch anyway. She doesn't have a real excuse like you do to avoid the task. You knew how to make Henry the manager feel just a little bit uncomfortable in the way you whispered, morning sickness throw-up, yes that would be bad for business. You fiddle with the condiments on the gray-speckled counter, the salt shaker next to the pepper shaker. Remember how, back when your biggest worry was finishing all of the broccoli on your plate so you could have dessert, you would marry the salt and the pepper, sliding them across the table to a hummed wedding march. Ketchup officiated. The fries cried into their tissues in the pews, and the hamburger threw a party afterwards where the pickles got drunk and the soda danced the electric slide. "Oh, hello. One foot-long, no sauerkraut, jumbo diet Pepsi? $3.85." The register reveals its inner secrets with an explosive eagerness, almost like one of those pop-up books you still secretly love. You hand back the change in coins, sliding them across the counter with the tips of your fingers, making sure to drag the pennies and nickels through half-congealed puddles of grease or sugar along the way. "Keep the change?

You sure?" You count the number of babies that pass by the restaurant's glass facade. They are suddenly everywhere. You think, my baby will be something special. Mustard. Straw. Napkin. You are less picky and more confused, really, as you store these words away, each a potential baby name.

II. SHOPPING LISTS
Tampons.
Bread.
Underwear.

Watermelon.
 No money. Shit.
Saltines.
A new man.

III. DRUGS I HAVE KNOWN
Who's to say I am a good girl, but I have never touched a drug. Not even Advil for headaches. Not pot or cocaine or heroin, and I am scared of needles, which means I don't have any tattoos either. I am clean. Except if I did get a tattoo, which I have not and would not, I would get one on my inner wrist. It would spell Believe.

IV. PRAYERS
Dear God, If you—I mean, You—know everything and all that, why do I have to take time and sit down and close my eyes ("Breathing deeply helps," Mr. Priest told me) and tell you all over again? Isn't that just wasting our time? But if I'm going to do this, I want to do it right. You know this. I want—the opposite of fear. I don't know what it's called. I just want to do what's right. I want to go to bed with dry eyes and a full stomach and a warm happiness all around. I want everyone to have these things. Even Kiley the fast-food bitch, because I guess

she's not a bitch to you—You—anyway. I want these fry burns to go away from my arms. I guess I want money, too. So my kid will never have these kinds of questions.

V. MONDAYS

Her water broke while she was on the bus, headed toward Heavenly Hotdogs. People were packed in tight on the downtown-bound 2A. The bus rocked and sped, ignorant, and soon people started surrendering to the slick floor. A chorus of disgruntled voices obscured what was important, the cries of girl who is contracting into womanhood. She never made it to the hospital. Were it not for an ex-cabbie who had experience in this sort of impromptu birthing, along with the help of several men and women who were parents and therefore understood the miracle of the impending event, the world might not have known a Papercup/Onionring/Milkshake Jones.

True story. But the child was named Junior.

EL QUATRO DE JULIO
MACKENZIE JACOBY, 16
WALDEN SCHOOL OF LIBERAL ARTS
PROVO, UT
TEACHER: LARA CANDLAND

This summer I spent three weeks in a tiny apartment in Barcelona, the heart of Catalonia, Spain. As important as space-time markers are in personal narratives, the real key to the previous sentence was the word "tiny." Allow me to elaborate. I shared a room with my sister. We are of notable heft, considerable bulk, we do not fit in a breadbox.

We slept on a double fold-out bed that, tiny though it was, proved too big to be folded out without hindering the movement of the door. By "hinder" I mean prevented the door from opening. In order to leave (or enter) the room, you had to lift up one end of the bed, open (and swiftly close) the door, and not think about recreating the process again for at least a couple of hours. Going to bed had a certain tone of finality to it.

We had been gone from the United States for seven months, and Europe had taken its toll on us. We began just as excited as can be to immerse ourselves in the European culture, and yet, seven months in we were soaked to the bone, soggy with savvy. Every night, when our bed had been folded out and our door had been closed, we dreamed of Nesquick, Jiffy peanut butter, even the friends that we had left behind. I had been going seven months strong and doing fine, but now with three weeks left, the amount of time I spent in dreams about home surpassed the amount of time I spent living. It was a very tiring existence. I even lost weight. Not enough that Taylor and I comfortably fit in the bed, but enough that it became visibly clear that I was burning more calories to keep up with my double life. And then, on the horizon, I saw the fourth of July. We all saw it. It was coming at us with amazing speed, we quickly calculated that when it arrived, we would still be here in Spain, cherubs mocking us from bedazzling architecture, the yawning language barrier rendering incomprehensible the chatter that surrounded us.

In Idaho, we have this cabin in the woods. Of course, that statement harbors, in its structure, a rather enormous reservoir of irony. Woods, and Cabin. Truer words have never been spoken; however, our own little Walden Pond, it is not. Owned by my grandparents (on my mother's side) and built by the paid labor of my dad and his hooligan brother, the cabin sits, with its seven bedrooms and fully equipped kitchen, a cushy 75-minute drive from Boise. It is built of roughly hewn logs though. The roof is red metal, the exterior is done in true Lincoln-log fashion, and there are carved bears and birch trees out front. Really, every necessary aspect of a good cabin is present, plus we have a ping-pong table.

So we needed a celebration: Obviously my first inclination was to find fireworks, but the thought was never verbalized as, being impossible, it would have made me look foolish. Food was the next best option. When being fed, people automatically assume they are having a great time. The person can be fully aware of what is going on without any negative effects, in fact on several occasions I've set myself up for such a trick, and have been thoroughly convinced that I was experiencing real hard-earned joy. So food was a must. A barbeque we would call it. We were on our way.

It's a six-hour drive to the cabin. We say we go up to water-ski, to four-wheel, to swim and fish, and even, to see our family. These explanations vary in levels of ludicrousness, from the believable to the laughable. But most family members find solace in one or two of the above reasons. The following insight is one that few of us have consciously noted, but it is the mantra of each of our souls. We go there to eat. We go there to eat "Grandma Terry's Trifle." Trifle is a curious thing, though curious is a word altogether too negative. Strange though it may be, trifle is perhaps the least offensive food known to man (the British don't like peanut-butter-and-jelly sandwiches). It involves creamy, soft, silky, soggy, many words but never chewy, layers and chunks of different ingredients that each, though eager to please, always complement and never bully their fellow tastes. It is a dish that bridges gaps, represents unity, and is easily digested.

It had to be made. At the time of course, we didn't write the recipe down, we knew what we needed. This is almost absolutely the first time that the following recipe has been written down because, more than a recipe, it is something that lives in our minds, something our intestines yearn for. Writing it down for any purpose but this would be fruitless, as our hands will disregard it in favor of what they know is right.

GRANDMA TERRY'S TRIFLE
INGREDIENTS:
> One Angel-Food Cake
> One pkg. of Strawberry Junket
> One pkg. of Vanilla Pudding (Jell-O brand, naturally)
> Blueberries
> Strawberries
> Raspberries
> One Pint of Whipped Cream

PROCEDURE:
Take a big, glass, cylindrical dish, for which I know no name. Breathe easy for a few moments and gather the confidence you need, but just know that scarce little can be done to ruin the dessert at this point. Start plopping in the various ingredients; only structure can hinder you at this point. Find a song and to its beat build your masterpiece, choose something soulful, but whose lyrics will not require analysis. Do not accept outside help and, if possible, tune out all noise around you. Your eyes are your biggest assets. Look at the colors. Have a good time.

Grocery Shopping was an epic journey. Our minds walked the logical path toward America, indulging in memories, getting hopes up, and visualizing the flawless outcome. Our feet, still based in Spain, struggled to keep up. The public transportation system made Pavlov's dogs of us. "Costco" was mentioned and made saliva well up in my mouth. We couldn't figure out the word for blueberry, the literal translation got less-than-coherent responses. And then the brightness attacked. Up until this point it had been something I was puzzled by and certainly at the mercy of, but something with which I could happily coexist. The sun didn't beat, our blaze, it was much more subtle; its heavy rays slowly seeped in from the top of my skull. By the time I realized what was happening, my ankles and calves had already been pushed down, submerged in the cement. I trudged along, dragging the sidewalk with me. Three hours and four grocery stores later, not one ingredient had been found in its intended form. Our standards were dropping quickly. Strawberries and bananas were decided on as the fruit portion, and a packaged but suitable substitute for angel food cake had been found. None of us wanted to think about what came next: strawberry junket.

I had never realized how patchy my foundation for tradition and culture were until I had to analyze what exactly Junket was, and what might make a suitable replacement. Strawberry junket is kind of like Jell-O. My mother tells me it's more of a glaze; the package tells me it's ever-so-versatile and can be served with almost anything in want of a gelatinous coating but as far as I know, none of these claims have ever been tested. As far as I know, ours is the only family who uses it. There are few powders these days that can honestly claim to hold families together. I would like to say, for the purposes of this narrative, that there is only one, but Kraft Mac n' Cheese does do its part. In any case, neither powdered life-form could be found in Spanish grocery stores.

It's easy to see where prejudice comes from. It's easy to; upon hearing that a huge population of the world lives without the words "bake" and "sprinkles," just assume that they don't have the same capacity for happiness. It's incredibly easy, almost unavoidable, after having tasted trifle with junket and trifle with jelly, to condemn a whole country for their lack of variety in the gelatin aisle. I'm not saying we did, I'm just saying it would have been easy . . .

If there is one thing that can be said for certain, it's that Europeans screw around with their dairy products. Granted, once the grocery store is navigated and the correct white liquids are identified, the final product tends to be tastier that any American equivalent, but the trauma of differentiating between heavy, double, clotted, pouring cream, in the end, always gives your creation a bittersweet twinge. So we decided on spray whipped cream, something that at this point, recognizable as it was, didn't even feel like settling.

TRIFLE DE CATALONIA

INGREDIENTS:

Packaged Madeline's (a little French pastry, stale in this case)
One pkg. of flan mix
Bananas
Strawberries
Strawberry jelly
One can of sprayable whipped cream (better safe than shelf-milk)

PROCEDURE:

Arrange as above but with eyes half-squinted and partially focused elsewhere. Refrigerate before serving.

Traveling is one of those things that'll just linger. It will sit there in your bloodstream, fogging everything up; coloring everything its biased hue, waiting to cling to something of importance. Until you place it, give it meaning, you have to be firm and say to it: you there, you give context to this part of my life. Otherwise it'll just run wild in your system, tainting everything with significance until you can't remember what you're supposed to enjoy and what you aren't.

I've still got some free radicals, some memories that I acquired before I learned how to put them in their place. You can feel them when your sensory imputers get all in a jumble. Or when someone hands you a glow-stick and immediately you feel like you should be having a great time. They congregate in a haze around certain things like push pops and sixlets, things that reek of a sentimentality that is not at all personal. But this memory knows exactly where it belongs.

We ate the trifle like fiends. Disoriented by effort and heat, we forgot to reduce the portion sizes and, for our family of five, we prepared for a family of 20. With every day the leftovers grew better, the whipped cream broke down, softening the flan mix, and the stale angel food cake steeped in jelly became entirely compliant. The fourth of July came and went, as did the three weeks that separated us from our transatlantic flight home. We stayed in Utah long enough (three days) to realize it was too hot before we made the six-hour drive to the cabin. My Grandma brought trifle. As I looked at it, it began to pulsate, fuzzy sunlight formed a halo around it, a flamenco beat oozed from its insides; nobody else noticed.

AS THIN OF SUBSTANCE AS THE AIR?

MATTHEW LLARENA, 17

MIAMI BEACH SENIOR HIGH SCHOOL
MIAMI BEACH, FL
TEACHER: JULIE KLEIN

She sweeps by sweetly, a demure smile on her face, her brown hair folding at her shoulders. In her quiet glance I see everything I desire reflected back at me. I have barely spoken to her and yet I have learned to love her gentle, throaty voice. My imagination has taken her innocent smile, rather attractive features, apparent intelligence, and, most important of all, her taciturn nature, and conjured the perfect person, my internal complement. Her friends seem pretentious, even obnoxious, and yet on some near-unconscious level I have decided that she is somehow different. Clearly I have caught my imagination and questioned it just before letting it run away with me, but despite logic I have been unable to quell the fluttering in my stomach that I feel with such intensity at this very moment as she passes. Even though I realize that I am awake, I cannot help but pursue the creations of my imagination, characters from dreams that are probably nothing more than aspects of myself, and even though I realize that I am superimposing eidetic images of my own invention on a quiet girl who has betrayed very few of her thoughts, I cannot help but allow my fantasies to seize me, on the off chance that I will encounter someone resembling the person I have created, an affirmation of the existence of the mind out of which I peer curiously.

I meet her eyes for a brief moment and then allow mine to fall to the floor. I am too shy to be looked at, too unsure of what she'll see. In one moment I swear that she is smiling at me and in the next I curse myself for thinking it, for wanting something that isn't there. She takes her seat. She is wearing corduroy again. The teacher calls on her to read her sonnet. She meekly whispers a soft string of words. "That was beautiful, Lacy," says Ms. Hardy, beaming at her. I am called on next. I don't have anything. Last night I became lost in complexity and eloquence eluded me. "A writer has but one lifetime, Aidan," jokes Ms. Hardy. "Just get it in next time." I return her smile weakly because I know that one night will never be long enough. Failed poets often make the best writers of prose because their writing comes compellingly close to recreating the reality of human experience that you feel an almost spiritual communion with their words. The blank page before them demands definition, demands that they bare their soul rather than trade the truthful conflict of their poetry for romantic delusions, for shameless lies. When I sit down to write, my thoughts inevitably drift to Lacy and then all understanding becomes obscured by the familiar ache of concupiscence. The bell rings and the class rushes to leave. She thoughtfully finishes a sentence and slips her notebook into her bag. As she slings the strap over her shoulder and blithely walks toward the door, I want desperately to make myself known to her.

"Hey," I call out too softly to be heard. It's too late . . . she has walked away before I can tell her how much I liked her poem.

I don't go straight home after school. Instead I take the long route to the park by the bay. I watch the pelicans floating in the breeze, falling from time to time into a graceful dive to catch a fish below. My mind defies the calm, returning to the words I wrote last night, to all that they are unable to express. I tried to write my poem about Lacy, but none of it made sense. It was an absurd assortment of abstractions that refused every word I wrote. I have felt this way before. I have wanted so badly to see an ideal realized that I convinced myself of its existence, only to see the beautiful illusion shattered, because it was never anything more than an image in a mirror. Still I struggle with these abstractions with the desperate hope that they will unfold into meaning. Still I find myself trying to translate the truth of all my sensitivity because it has always seemed possessed of such profoundness.

A hand on my shoulder disrupts my thought suddenly and I jump in response. "Relax," says Michael, laughing, "I'm not trying to steal your wallet." He runs his hand through his greasy blond hair with a sly, almost mocking grin stretched across his face. "I saw you sitting here all alone and I thought I'd bring you a surprise."

I know what it is before he takes it out, and I know that even after having gone a few months without it, I won't refuse.

"I was just about to find myself a little spot to light this up, and then I saw you sitting over here and decided to make your day," he says as he sits beside me, looks around and, seeing no one, lights his joint.

He passes it to me and exhales. I take a deep drag and hold it in. When I first started smoking, I decided that there couldn't possibly be anything wrong with the gentle relief the pleasure allowed me. It felt as though I had found all the comfort, all the understanding that seemed to have been forgotten by the world around me. Slowly, subtly, it wove itself into my psyche. It became the only thing that I believed in, and I clung to it the way I had always clung to ideals. The more I smoked, the more I found the world inside my head to be irreconcilable with the one around me and tried desperately to escape it. The illusion fell apart, and just like all of the other illusions my mind had conjured, it left me all the more alone, all the more lost. In my withdrawal I retreated to the familiar safety of introspection. I began to read voraciously. I went to the library every day and poured over novels, books on philosophy and poetry. I savored the wondrous beauty of reality. It was months before I smoked again. Even though my will to discover meaning has kept me from returning fully, I still have these moments of uncertainty. I pass the joint to Michael.

"I heard you dropped out," I say to Michael.

"Yeah, that place wasn't doing shit for me. I moved out of my house too. I've got my own apartment now. All I do is chill and smoke."

He flashes me that same sly grin and I catch his eye as he passes me the joint. I remember catching his eye just like this a long time ago, when we were younger, before we had passed joints between us. I remember seeing his eyes fill with light like two blue stained-glass windows. Now, as he quickly looks away, I see nothing of that light. I want to say something meaningful to him, to reason with him, but no words come to me. My body begins to flood with pleasure and feel heavy as I pass him the joint. A moment later he flicks the roach onto the ground, says that he really should be going and begins to walk away. I sit on my bench until the water rises and turns a deep orange color.

Lacy's eyes, light brown like her hair, seem to glimmer with receptivity whenever I work up the nerve to say something to her. She smiles at my jokes, even those I tell to whomever happens to be sitting beside me in class in hopes that she will overhear. I think of almost nothing else as I make my way home, catching myself for a moment before continuing my reverie: I must accept that it is more likely than not that she, too, is an illusion. How dangerous it is to hope, to allow myself even to consider the possibility that I have perceived the truth of who she is intuitively. It occurs to me that she would probably be repulsed by everything I've done today: my pathetic, longing call, my smoking, my whole preoccupation with her. More often than not, when this happens to me, when I build someone up in my mind and finally ask them out, full of expectation, they sense my delusion and are repelled by all the conflict within me. They see the way I look at them, my eyes filled with a supplicating light, and somehow they know that it's not them I love, but something I have projected onto them, something I've been looking for all of my life in one form or another. Sometimes they touch my arm, bat their eyelashes, tell me how important I've become to them, and then when the moment of expectation comes, the illusion is shattered and for all I know I imagined the whole thing. But when I look into Lacy's eyes I cannot believe that she would be repulsed because they seem full of such understanding. I suppose that's easy to believe when you want it to be true, and when the person has yet to say anything to contradict your image of them.

The screen door bounces against its frame three times before it finally clicks shut behind me. There is a plate of chicken and rice on the table. Mom must be going out again. Several dresses are laid out on the sofa with a few pairs of heels on the floor below them. She emerges from the bathroom, curlers in hair, lipstick in hand. She smiles, kisses me on the cheek and continues changing frantically. She asks about my day and complains when I offer limited responses. I sit on the couch and avoid her eyes. A car pulls up outside just as she slips her heels on. I kiss her goodnight, glad that she finished readying herself in time, relieving me of an awkward encounter with her date. "Well, I'll be back by eleven. Your dinner is on the table. Love you."

I take my stuff into the bedroom, which is divided in two by a sheet hanging from the ceiling. When we moved in she insisted that I take the bedroom, arguing that I was going to need a quiet place to study. She said that she would be comfortable enough with a room divider in the living room. Her eyes used to fill with tears when I brought home straight A's. She would go on about how I was going to have a wonderful job, be a good man, marry the perfect girl, have children and be happy. She has always given me more credit than I deserve. While I liked to see her as happy as she was when she was fantasizing about my future, there was something about those tears that filled me with a terrible anxiety. In the year I stopped caring about those stupid letters on a piece of paper, because I decided that they had no meaning, I stopped showing her my grades and she didn't say a word. She preferred to pretend that nothing had changed. She caught me smoking that year and she wept disconsolately, shrieking, completely unwilling to listen to my feeble attempts to explain. When I looked at her, I was overwhelmed by that same terrible anxiety and promised I would stop. And then it was over. She looked tired the next day, but she smiled at me, preferring to pretend that the whole thing had been some sort of bad dream.

She goes out several times a week, trying to find someone who will love her. The hair dye she uses to keep the gray from showing and the creams she uses to hide her wrinkles sit on her nightstand. She cannot help but believe in love. She cannot help but believe that if she is a good person, then there is no conceivable reason why life should not bring her love. And even though the truth of her life seems to contradict her philosophy, even though it seems likely that her belief is an awful form of self-deception, she cannot question any of it because losing faith in love would mean losing faith in life. "Finding a man will make it all better," she tells herself. She lives for that moment that will confirm that her many years of unwavering faith in love were not wasted. I think of what it must have been like when she was 20, pregnant and in college, when my father left her, and I can't feel anything but pity for her. I came up with the idea of sharing the bedroom. You have to pass through her side to get to mine. She gets the closet and I get a quiet place to study.

I lie down on my bed for a while and then move to the living room to do the same on the couch. I can't imagine bringing Lacy here, sitting with her on this ratty second-hand furniture in front of this T.V. that doesn't get any channels. Maybe she's like me and doesn't like T.V. anyway. I eat and then grab my notebook in hopes of producing a poem. I turn Lacy's words around inside my head.

The assignment was to write a sonnet and Ms. Hardy said that if we were moved to write something romantic, as we have been reading Romeo and Juliet, all the better. Before Juliet, Romeo loved Rosaline. If you could ask Romeo whether or not his feelings for Juliet were true love, he would tell you yes; but if you could ask Shakespeare, he would tell you that both wanted love so badly that they imagined themselves in the other. Both were lucky—debatably, not so lucky—to have found someone just as deluded as themselves. No one intelligent enough to craft Romeo's emphatic vows of love would be as ignorant of his condition as he. I have never known what to tell a girl and have always made a fool out of myself. "It is the east and Juliet is the sun," whispers an idealistic cynic from above. I have no one to whisper brilliant lines in my ear. There is only my own internal monologue.

My lower lip gently draws Lacy's further into the kiss. I am aware that we are somewhere in school, but the intensely pleasurable tension that fills my body dims that awareness. My hands run up the arch of her back, pulling her toward me. I feel a tremble escape my control. It flows from my body into hers like an electrical current. My eyes open suddenly. The sharp sound of a lock clicking into place and a key being drawn from it wake me. Mom must be leaving for work. I am still on the couch. I realize that I didn't finish any of my homework. There is a quilt wrapped around me. How strange, how incredibly absurd it is to be having such tender dreams about someone who is essentially a stranger! My alarm clock beeps loudly in my room and I get up to shut it off. Breakfast is on the table: scrambled eggs, fruit, and tea.

I shower, dress, eat, and walk to school. I don't pay much attention in my first period. When I get to Ms. Hardy's class I walk quickly to the back of the room. She doesn't ask me for my poem. Lacy walks in and I imagine her merging with her dream counterpart that so willingly embraced me. She takes a seat in the row to the left of mine a few seats up. Ms. Hardy begins class, but I continue to stare at Lacy. "I hope everyone brought their books today . . . " Lacy turns around suddenly, looking directly at me as though she had felt my eyes on her. I turn awkwardly to look at Ms. Hardy who begins read from the scene with Mercutio's famous rant about Queen Mab and dreams:

True I talk of dreams,

Which are the children of an idle brain, Begot of nothing but vain fantasy; Which is as thin of substance as the air . . .

She stops there. "Some critics have argued that it is in these lines that Shakespeare comes fully to the surface, using Mercutio to express his belief that all that comes to pass between Romeo and Juliet is nothing more than the playing out of "vain fantasy." After having read this play, what do you think? Do think that it is through Mercutio that Shakespeare speaks to us?" She looks around for someone to call on. My heart sinks as her eyes come to rest on me. "Aidan, what do you think?"

I look at my desk for a moment, wanting to disappear. Sentences start to form themselves and I begin to speak. "No, I don't agree with that. Mercutio is the defiant, vulgar, witty, colorful character that he is because he believes that dreams are 'as thin of substance as the air.' On a deeper level, his wit is his attempt to create meaning within the meaningless dream that is reality . . . he makes puns even as he is dying as a last act of defiance against the madness of meaninglessness. Shakespeare kills Mercutio to show us that he is as flawed in his philosophy as Romeo, because believing that the world holds no meaning is just as emotional of a response to life as blindly believing that it is full of meaning."

Ms. Hardy beams at me the way she beamed at Lacy the day before. I don't listen much for the rest of class. I am not nearly as certain as Romeo and Mercutio. I look at Lacy. I cannot feel love, or anything for that matter, without questioning it. The bell rings and I resolve to defy all of my uncertainty and speak with her because even though I can never hope to receive a definite answer, it is the only way to test the nature of dreams. I move toward her as she makes her way to the door. I have no idea what I will say, but I feel as though Fate is forcing me in her direction.

"Aidan," Ms. Hardy calls, motioning me to her desk. Lacy walks away, again . . . Ms. Hardy tells me that my grades have been slipping due to my failure to turn in assignments. "Do not squander your intelligence," she says. I apologize and tell her that I have had a lot on my mind. She offers me her ear should I ever want to speak to her.

I walk to the park after school. How ironic it is that every moment demands that we react, and yet we are deprived of the meaning of the interaction. I sit on the seawall and watch the undulating flow beneath me. The light plays upon the water's surface, shimmering brilliantly as it merges with its own reflection. I remember an experiment I read about that proves that electrons are both waves and particles. They are only particles when they come into contact with a conscious observer. The rest of the time they are waves of possibility, potential matter. Some quantum physicists assert that because the manifestation of the material world is dependent on a conscious observer, consciousness is more fundamental than matter. Others disagree that it is consciousness exactly that is collapsing electrons into physical reality, but it seems that no matter what you call it, some essential aspect of the observer is more fundamental than matter. But what do I know? I'm not very good at math. I read a book by a physicist that said that quantum mechanics is suggesting what Buddhism has been professing for thousands of years: that the divide between what is within and what is without is an illusion. He meditates for hours to detach himself from this illusion of isolation for a momentary glimpse of reality as it is on the deepest level of truth: consciousness permeated by a sea of infinite possibilities. I would love nothing more than to watch logic unfold into a sea of infinite possibilities. I'll probably never be able to do the calculations, but is not poetry a system of symbols as well? Einstein dreamt of writing an equation to talk to God, of seeing his symbols reveal all the meaning he had been searching for his whole life.

I get home and find immense vulnerability and complexity spilling from me. I struggle with the structure, but after an hour or so I look down at the page, riddled with markings and crossed out lines, and see my finished sonnet scribbled in the corner.

Before I know it, I am in front of the class, preparing to read my poem. I look over at Lacy and delight in her apparent receptivity, imagined or not. Perhaps after I read, I will find that no one understood a word I wrote—it has happened before—but I will continue to try to translate these abstractions because I can't deny the feeling that they hold some sort of profound meaning and I know nothing beyond what I feel. When I finish reading I look directly into Lacy's eyes, she looks back smiling, and I know that today I will catch her before she walks out the door.

BENEATH THE SNOW: A MEMOIR

ERIC KOFMAN, 16

CARY ACADEMY
CARY, NC
TEACHER: PALMER SEELEY

The photograph was displayed prominently in the entry to my grandparents' ski cabin in Chile, behind a veil of glass in a thick wooden frame. It was one of the cherished trophies that lined the walls of the log cabin in La Parva, where we spent our winter weekends. My father and uncle's ski medals shimmered on the dark felt boards over the fireplace, neatly ordered in a matrix of silver, gold and bronze. The photograph hung right over the door, waiting for acknowledgement each time I came in from the snow-covered deck; I always had plenty of time to ponder it while I stomped the white chunks off my shoes. Though its significance was not clear to me, its place among the other recognizable prizes conveyed its importance.

There were two people in the photo, each seated on opposite sides of a narrow table and facing the other. On the right flank sat my grandfather, León, but with his jowls tighter and eyes brighter than those of the León I knew as a seven-year-old. His left hand, elevated with fingers spread, firmly accentuated his words. I didn't know who the other man in the image might be. He had white hair and a thin white mustache that lined his upper lip, and he wore a magnificent white military suit with gold buttons; he was resting his arms on the table and leaning across them.

"Who is that man in white?" I asked León one afternoon, as he reclined in his chair after a good day of skiing. He lifted his chin from his neck to look where I pointed.

"That man," he said, his fingers releasing the remote control and extending a bit shakily, "saved Chile from falling to pieces. His name is Augusto Pinochet. If it hadn't been for General Pinochet, Chile would be a ruined country today." His hand hammered down into his thigh as he tried to make clear to me how important this man was. León's rotary club had been honored by the General's visit, and it was this meeting that had been captured in the still image enshrined in the little cabin in La Parva.

So this man was a hero. That made sense; he was a prince just like in the Disney videos I watched all the time, a savior in white arriving just in time to save the kingdom. That's the extent to which my seven-year-old mind extrapolated its first lesson in politics.

■

Still, I couldn't see how the Chile that I lived in could ever have been so close to falling apart. My Chile was stable, and I woke up every day at seven in the morning to go to Nido de Aguilas with my second-grade friends.

My favorite class was art with Mr. Leo, who looked like a monkey, with a thin nose and arched eyebrows that scrunched over narrow eyes. He was so enthusiastic about his job that he often forgot that the art-work that he enjoyed critiquing so much had been created by seven-year-old children. However, I didn't notice his biting criticism until the day we drew clowns. Mr. Leo walked up and down with clicking steps in the space between the two long tables where we all sat hunched over our sheets, listening to the footsteps. His paces marked the drumming waltz of an army sergeant and they stopped behind me; I waited expec-tantly, hoping for praise. I had drawn a great clown with blues, purples and yellows, but I especially loved the nose. Noses are impossible to draw, almost as difficult as ears, but you can leave out the ears without having a clown look strange. I hoped Mr. Leo would like my nose too; his verdict was the final judgment. "Eric," he said, in a quiet but commanding voice, "Clowns have round noses." His clacking steps continued their drumbeat down the floor, and I sadly began erasing my wonderful nose.`

Starting that second-grade year, I played soccer after school three days a week. Chile was all about soccer. Although the Chilean teams never could quite compete with too many other countries, they were unwaveringly the pride of every Chilean. Every little kid played. Having inherited a single Chilean soccer gene from just my dad (my mom is American), I wasn't great at it. The ball always escaped from my foot to find a more experienced cleat. The third and fourth graders monopolized the field, so I never got a chance to improve; I went anyways, resentfully, because my mom thought it would be good for me.

There were several heroic players of amazing skill on our team to whom we all looked up: José-Maria, Manuel, and Rafael. They were only a grade ahead of us, but towered over us second graders. We all idolized them and wished we could play as well as they did.

■

I didn't understand what could cause a country to crumble: I wasn't versed at all in history, and politics was a sphere that wouldn't even begin to interest me for another five years. What does it mean for a country to be "ruined"? I turned to my dad for an explanation, and he gave me his stories.

He explained that Salvador Allende was elected president of Chile in 1970, at the lowest point of a depression that had made an already poor country even more destitute. He was a Marxist, and had promised better times for the impoverished segment of the population, which represented a lot of people at that time. One of his first actions was controlling prices. This was initially good for people with less money, but for the business owners, it was a disaster: the prices Allende set were hardly enough to cover the costs of production. It didn't make sense to sell anything anymore, and little by little, thousands of businesses, small and big, were effaced from the map. The workers took over the factories, but couldn't operate them because they couldn't get credit or supplies. Eventually, Chile lost any self-sufficiency it had had. The peso was nearly worthless. The government had to import products donated from other communist countries; cans of Polish beans and packs of Russian meat floated around. Resources were scarce.

My dad was about 18 years old when he saw Chile's economy trashed by communism in less than a year. His middle-class family was denied rations of meat, which were exclusively reserved for the poor. There were no other means of procuring meat. One day he was walking around in a poorer section of town when a man came up to him and whispered a question: "Do you want to buy some meat?" he asked. "Be here at four in the morning before my line gets too long." So my dad woke up in the middle of the freezing winter night to buy meat on the black market. There was already a line forming of about 30 people bundled in overcoats. My dad bought what would have been a whole cow and took it home—his family used that meat for four months.

My dad told me about his grandmother Esther, who had fled to Chile from Russia in the '20s when Lenin took over. Her family had lost almost everything back in the old country. Now in her 70s, she was terrified of the new communist leadership, and sold every asset she owned before she could lose them all over again. "Oy-Vey! I've seen this before," she would exclaim, "Oy-Vey!"

General Augusto Pinochet saved the day. Chile's hero came in and destroyed the villain. A military coup took Allende out in 1973; the police, the army, the navy, and the air force all were in on the plot and Allende was dead by the time it was over—many people said it was by his own hand.

My dad explained that Pinochet was a polarizing figure. Half the country loved him and half the country despised him. No one could argue that Chile under his rule didn't become the economic miracle it's so often called today. He was dictator for more than 15 years, but brought the country to new heights: the man in white saved Chile.

■

While waiting for the soccer coach to arrive, we would throw paper planes. That was the official activity for us second-grade boys. The newest novelty was a model that a chubby kid in my class, Juan, brought to school one day and taught us how to make. We would all fold our "divers" and throw them around. They would meander through the air above our heads and dance toward the ground slowly, seeming as though they would never come down. Then their white tips would plow into the ground.

One day, we were tossing our planes and watching them spiral down, when suddenly José-Maria walked in and stepped on mine. I watched, frozen, as his foot crushed the paper. He lifted his foot off and stepped back, so I ran in to retrieve my wreckage. Suddenly I was thrown to the ground by heavy hands and José-Maria was laughing and so were Manuel and Rafael. The hero of our team had just knocked me down and was laughing about it. From my view on the ground the three third graders looked more powerful than ever, and my back hurt. My plane was smashed and brown and half-buried in the dirt.

■

The road down from La Parva was long and winding. "Curva 92" said the yellow sign at the top. Only 91 hairpin turns on the edge of a cliff remaining. From the high vantage point, I could see the cloud of smog hovering over Santiago; it smothered the buildings like a carpet. I settled in for the long ride ahead and asked my dad to tell me more stories about Pinochet and Chile.

He was quiet for a little as he stared past the steering wheel. Then he said, "You know, Eric, some people say that everyone has a little bit of bad inside them. They also say that this badness takes over when someone has power. When people have absolute power, which is what Pinochet had, they can do some really bad things, just because they think they can get away with it." He told me about the three thousand people who "disappeared" in the few months following the coup. He told me about the rounding up of unarmed leftists. He told me of the people who were tortured, and the $30 million Pinochet had sneakily stashed offshore. He explained how my grandmother's brother, Nano, was tossed into the Estadio while he had a stomach ulcer just because his wife attended leftist meetings. If my grandmother hadn't been able to find him and get him out as soon as she did, he would have died within a few days. Pinochet was responsible for these terrible "crimes against humanity." Had he been content with deposing Allende's communist and corrupt government, he'd be referred to as a hero; as it was, most people consider him a brutal dictator. It's a fine line, and he crossed it by allowing the power to go to his head.

So the hero was the villain. His good deeds were in the shadow of his darker ones, and things weren't black and white in my mind anymore. Poor, sick 80-year-old man who had saved the country; and former dictator, "embodiment of brutality," corrupt criminal against humanity—how could both be so true?

We finally reached the foothills after an eternity of continuous turns. The snow that had blanketed the ground and frosted the rocks outside the windows for the past hour had given way to a dusty dirt road; the brown weeds and the cacti stood out in sharp contrast to the smooth whiteness on the mountain tops. We were still on the mountain, but far from those towering peaks, seeing a different facet of the Andes: the coarse dirt beneath the snow. The road slid past a creek swirling with brown water that ran quickly, almost ashamedly, from its pristine source and disappeared ahead, into the shroud of smog enveloping Santiago.

THE TRANSFORMATION
ELIZABETH COZART, 17
CEDAR FALLS HIGH SCHOOL
CEDAR FALLS, IA
TEACHER: JENNIFER PAULSEN

At 5:15 p.m., central daylight time, when the sky abruptly turned from its everyday blue to a vivid, luminous orange, Lily did not see the transformation, because she was sitting in her bedroom facing her floor-length mirror, attempting to master the art of ventriloquism. One of Lily's dearest dreams was to be a ventriloquist, if only a tolerable one. "I like cake," she said to her mirror. "Do you like cake?" But as she said "do," her lower lip invariably moved, and she gave an exasperated sigh. It was at that moment that the sky changed color, and Lily, who was struggling to pronounce "do" without moving her lips, heard the sound of screeching tires outside her window, several screams and/or shrieks, and a furious chorus of barking. (The dogs, of course, were barking because dogs see the world in shades of blue and yellow, and they, too, had witnessed the transformation.)

Lily rose slowly and went to the window. She saw a dozen faces raised to the sky and her next-door neighbor, Mrs. Peterson, standing in her yard with both hands clasped over her mouth, as if someone had uttered a frightful obscenity. And then, looking up, Lily saw what they saw. It was, she thought, the same color as the peel of a ripe tangerine.

The next few days were madness. It's the terrorists, some said; it's the apocalypse, said others. It's impossible, said the scientists. Whatever the cause, people seemed incapable of functioning normally with the sky such an unusual shade. A national emergency was declared, and no one went to work. People huddled in their houses, or filled their cellars with food, or flipped frantically through the Book of Revelation searching for precedents; some merely stood in their backyards, heads tilted back, watching, waiting, as if hoping what had happened would reverse itself just as suddenly as it had occurred.

One evening, as the sun was setting and the sky was darkening from a burnt orange to a dark chocolate, Lily sat watching the evening news. Her hair was held up in a twist by two number two pencils, and she was chewing absentmindedly on a third. On the screen, a number of well-known scientists were arguing: "As of yet, we have found no physical change in the composition of the sky," declared the one from Oxford, only to be interrupted by the professor from Harvard who said caustically, "If you haven't noticed, the sky turned orange—obviously there must be a change in its composition." Whereupon the scientist from Princeton pointed out, "Any change in composition most likely would have been the result of a long, gradual process, not an abrupt transformation . . . honestly, I don't see why everyone's so upset, I think it's a perfectly lovely color . . . "

Lily thought this opinion was the most reasonable and wanted to hear him continue, but, at this point, the screen flickered, pixilated until it looked like an Impressionist-era work of pointillism, and then cut to footage of a mass protest in Germany, where thousands of people marched the streets, demanding that the sky be returned to its natural color. After a minute, the screen flickered once more, and when it recovered, the marchers had been replaced by a famous poet. Leaning intently toward the camera, her frizzy hair a halo around her head, her eyes stretched wide, she whispered, "It's a symbol—orange is the color of warning—we are being warned."

The days passed, and the sky remained impossibly, inexplicably, unapologetically orange. People gradually were returning to work, having apparently accepted that nothing could be done about the transformation, and life was returning to something resembling the norm. Lily continued to practice her ventriloquism before her floor-length mirror, and the scientists fruitlessly continued to search the skies for answers. At 4:12 p.m., central daylight time, on a Monday, Lily's mother stood at the base of the stairs and hollered, for perhaps the tenth time, "Lily, take out the trash!" Lily, who, with great concentration and perseverance, had been trying to say "please pass the cake" without moving her lips, bellowed, "Alright, already!" She got to her feet and thundered down the stairs, grabbed the bag of trash from the kitchen, and marched out to the end of the driveway. As she stuffed the plastic bag into its bin, something amazing happened: every single blade of grass in her yard, and every single blade of grass in Mrs. Peterson's yard, and every single blade of grass for as far as she could see, instantaneously turned a dazzling, startling _____. (Unfortunately this color has no name, because it is a color that has never been seen before and cannot be created by any mixture of paints or be seen in any realm of the atomic emission spectra. But no matter, I assure you it was a most marvelous color and contrasted well with the orange sky.) And Mrs. Peterson, who was mowing her lawn next door, gave a shrill and equally marvelous ear-splitting scream.

SLIP ROAD
CLEO O'BRIEN-UDRY, 15

ACES EDUCATIONAL CENTER FOR THE ARTS
NEW HAVEN, CT
TEACHER: CAROL ROSENSTONE

I was cut out of my mother's womb by a C-section as the subways of Chicago were evacuated, as fish-filled water spilled through the Chicago underground from a car-sized hole that had been punched through the bed of the Chicago River. The water still slid into basements beneath the silent streets as we drove home from the hospital in the Volkswagen. I crawled nude on the Persian carpet of our apartment, and I flew halfway around the world on rug-burnt knees, coming back to Chicago. Soon we moved to Ghana—where my parents had begun their courtship, riding together on the back of a motorcycle. We lived there for a year with the Jetta and a car dubbed the Beast.

We bought the Toyota in New Haven when we moved to the green house with two sets of wooden staircases that wound up like springs. The Toyota smelled of grass and dirt and sweat ground into the grainy carpet, and we never once used pine-scented taxi air-fresheners to cover that musty smell up. The highway was an adventure in the Toyota: the stick shift stuck in first gear, the thick grinding of tires against thin side metal, the manual windows stuck an inch from the top. I would stick my head out the window and catch the wind full on until my dad pulled me back into the car and seat-belted me tight. I watched the tire skids and oil leaks trail over the dotted white lines until they blurred into the black tar pavement, and sometimes I wondered who had driven those cars over the edge.

I couldn't sit in the passenger seat of most cars for fear that my lungs would be crushed if an air-bag exploded. The Toyota had no air-bags, so I could sit up front. My dad made me hold the map when we went on road trips; I was always several streets behind in the directions, and I didn't care whether we went right or left. I misled two carloads of people in Iowa and we got lost among the endless corn fields and cracked, unnamed roads for an hour. I was the only person who didn't mind. We tried renting a car with a GPS in Ohio, but the GPS broke and I didn't want to fix it.

We got lost in Cairo with a taxi driver who spoke no English, and we almost got hit when he pulled over to ask directions. The drivers never stopped shouting out of windows, never stopped driving even when the cars trafficked themselves into corners of the road. The cars brushed up against one another like strangers on the street, stuck on the highway until the traffic broke like a flood wall and the cars shot off like bullets. My mom was terrified. I loved it.

I spent the 12-hour flight back from Cairo staring out the window at the highways that spindled like veins across the fields below. Water streamed past my window, beaded on glass and flew off in fluid strips. Sleep was unnecessary with the world flying by.

A taxi picked us up at JFK airport to take us home after our flight docked at the gate. The Toyota was too small to fit our baggage, and even the minivan was too much of a hassle to take to the airport. Our taxi driver was a pleasantly enormous woman named Cookie who liked to talk and who laughed in a high-pitched whine that came in short bursts. Her brother was mentally disabled and her mother had Alzheimer's disease and an old man died at her house before she could give him CPR. She never stopped talking. An EasyPass on her window allowed her to speed through highway tollbooths.

The highway is the same height as the Ralph Walker Ice Skating Rink, where I learned to ride a two-wheeler. On the pebbled path in the back, I wheeled through the tangled crabgrass, knees bloody from falling. I wobbled across the empty football field, leaving a heap of dirty white training wheels in my wake. My dad ran beside me to balance my bumpy ride, setting me back up when I fell and pushing me forward when I got back up to try again.

My dad rides bikes constantly, even using a stationary bike to burn calories at home. I can't stand how that bike doesn't move; how I can peddle forward for hours and nothing changes, how my legs feel tired from moving but I'm still in my house, still in my living room, still looking at those cracks in the ceiling and that empty water bottle by the window. I go for runs around New Haven in shorts-and-T-shirt weather. I don't stop for cars, and when they don't stop for me, I turn the corner and go in loops around the block. My dad tells me he hates running without a destination.

After my dad was hit by a car while riding his bike, I thought I'd never get on a bike again. An old lady ran the stop sign three blocks down from our house and he was thrown up against the windshield. I thought he was going to die. He broke a couple of ribs and had to breathe from a tube in his lung, but he didn't let on that it hurt, and always smiled when we visited him in his hospital bed. He couldn't bike for weeks and drove the Toyota everywhere. My dad got a new bike after he recovered, silver with a hula-girl squeeze-toy that swishes her hips back and forth as he bikes. He rides this bike to work every day.

Almost two years after my dad's accident, we got a phone call from my aunt. I could tell it was bad when my mom stopped moving around while she talked. My cousin Jon had committed suicide. My aunt left for work that morning, and Jon locked himself in the garage, turned on the car and suffocated to death from its fumes. Before he died, he texted his friends, "See you on the other side." Jon must have had to sit in that motionless car for hours as he waited for the smoke to clog up his lungs like wet cement. I keep thinking that if only he had gotten up and out of the car or driven it out of the enclosed garage, he would still be alive.

My aunt got rid of the car before the funeral. No one knew where it was or dared to ask. We all sat, still and quiet with hands folded, not knowing what to say. Several months after the funeral, my parents proposed selling the Toyota. I cried and threatened to chain myself to the car and sit on the hood for days to make sure they knew if they gave away the Toyota they'd be losing their own daughter. My parents sold the Toyota. The new car is tan and clean with automatic pickup on highways. I sit with my feet on the dashboard and look out the window, but the road is too far down to watch the pavement passing by.

STEPS TO WORLD DOMINATION

PAUL MELCHER, 14

ST. JOHN'S SCHOOL
HOUSTON, TX
TEACHER: SHARON FABRIZ

THE FOLLOWING PROGRAM HAS BEEN APPROVED BY THE FCC FOR ALL AUDIENCE. PLEASE SILENCE YOUR CELL PHONE, PAGERS, BABIES, TIME BOMBS, AND YOUR EVIL ROBOT NINJA SQUADS. FEDERAL LAW PROHIBITS RECORDING AND SELLING THIS TAPE, BUT YOU'RE EVIL, SO YOU DON'T CARE. (MEET ME IN THE ALLEY AFTER THE PRESENTATION.)

Hello, fellow evildoer/psychotic villain/malicious clone/hateful twin/disgruntled postal worker/real estate agent. You are about to learn how to dominate the world. But first, you need a motive, something to keep you going even when things are not going so well. Several good motives include revenge, sticking it to the man, getting back at the DMV for making you wait in that long line that totally took forever, and then you're like, "Dude, turn on the air-conditioning or a fan or something." By utilizing these and other motives, you can climb to the top in no time.

Once you have your motive, it's time that you get an evil lair. Any of the following locations is acceptable: a remote island, a volcano, underneath a remote island's volcano, or most likely of all, your parents' basement. Remember that your parents might not like your putting up barbed wire all over the place, so get them out of the house, send them on a cruise, send them on a second honeymoon in Italy, or send them to Vegas; they really deserve a vacation. Do no blast them into space. Remember, you may be evil, but you're not going to be a jerk.

Now that you have your lair, it's time to get some funding for your evil plans; you can hire a goon to steal for you/sell stuff on the black market/rob an armored car/steal an old lady's purse/mooch off your parents. Remember, old ladies usually carry around candy in their purses—all the more reason to rob them. Try not to draw too much attention to yourself just yet; you're not ready for it.

Now that you have some funding, it's time to upgrade your lair. By this time you should have moved our of your parents' basement and if you haven't, then GET MOVING, the world isn't going to dominate itself. Some basic upgrades include gun racks, guard towers, missile defense systems, anti-air guns, flack cannons, sharks with laser beams strapped to their foreheads, and probably most important, SPIKES IN THE AIR DUCTS. Nothing says vulnerable like an empty air duct shaft. Don't forget to focus on the essentials. You NEED a conference table, a big remote-controlled arm chair, and a giant map of the world in the room where you plot your evil plans. Remember, a lair doesn't run itself; you will need electricians, janitors, and random equipment that has no apparent use or function.

Now that you are cozy, it's time to get evil. You will need henchmen and goons. See to it that your lair is crawling with them. You are also going to need a weapons cache. Build an armory and fill it with explosives, guns, combat vehicles and, if at all possible, a bunch of rocket launchers. Make sure that you get all the necessary ammunition; you don't want to look foolish while you try to destroy a bank now do you? Start building hordes of evil robot ninja death squads; they will be handy later, and they also look really cool. Finally, make sure your henchmen are trained for hand-to-hand and weapons combat. Nothing says incompetent overlord like a goon who cannot distinguish between a radio and a hand grenade. Also, make a doomsday device; it can give you a lot of political leverage.

Now that you are ready, it's time to make your evil debut. You might want to blow something up, steal a rally big gem, rob a big bank, rob and blow up Fort Knox, steal a whole bunch of hydrogen bombs, send out evil postcards of DOOM. Important: Make sure you have a good name; you can't have an evil organization without a good name.

Now it's time to put on a show. Hire someone to be your arch nemesis. Have him spoil your evil plans. This puts the general public into a false sense of security. It also gives you lots of publicity. Publicity can really get you places, and it makes getting ransom money easy. Some ways to gain publicity include destroying a bank, the moon, humanity, North Dakota. As an alternative, you can make a Broadway production.

Now it's time to dominate the world. First, release your horde of evil robot ninjas upon the world, and then swarm your goons all over the map. While you do this, bomb the armies of every nation within range. Give them no chance to retaliate. Put yourself in power and eliminate every other government. If you fail to take control, have your "nemesis" "foil" you and go into hiding so you can get more cash and start over. If you do establish a foothold, fortify it before anyone can stop you. You might want to build a Death Star of some sort.

Now that you have dominated the world, it's time to thing bigger. You now have the capabilities to conquer the universe, or you can clone yourself, or you could move out of your parents' basement. Seriously, man, I mean, come on.

Thus concludes this walkthrough on WORLD DOMINATION. To research this exciting field further, visit your local library, then steal all the books you need. And remember, knowledge is power, but hordes of evil robot ninjas are more powerful.

THE TEA EGG
XINHE SHEN, 16

MONTE VISTA HIGH
DANVILLE, CA
TEACHER: BARBARA BUCKLEY

The train ride didn't disappoint her.

The train chug-chug-chugged like it was supposed to, and the floors vibrated. She sat in the hard seat and clutched her bag—soft cloth, dark blue, dyed by the factory next to the village. Inside its indigo stomach, there was a change of clothes, toothpaste, thin corn wafers, her residency identification, and a letter her mother wrote to her uncle. Her 100-yuan bills were sewn into the lining of her underwear. She felt a swell of pride as she thought of her heavy responsibility.

Her mother warned her against thieves, so she clutched her bag as she slept on the train. She slept, and clutched, and cracked open her eyes to check if it was still there, and she didn't sleep well.

She awoke at sunrise, her stomach growling, the train coming to a stop. She saw a station with new concrete.

Her stomach grumbled again. The woman next to her started, shifted, and went back to sleep. Out the glass windows of the train, she could see the stocky man who sold tea eggs. His big tin pot overflowed with eggs the color of burnt umber, and with darkly stained cracks in their shells. The black-brown tea, in which they were submersed, exhaled thick white steam, wispy and warm against the cold, gray morning.

Mouth watering, stomach turning sour with hunger, she felt inside her soft cloth bag for the corn wafers. They were crisp and thin like paper, made of cornmeal crushed over and over again until it was the finest it could be. They tasted like paper, too. As she ate, she watched the tea-egg vendor outside the window artfully tend to his customers.

One female customer tried to pick up the eggs from the pot and jumped back, waving her burnt, red fingers in the air like a quick fan. The vendor brought out a plastic bag and, one by one, picked the piping hot eggs from the pot and placed them in the bag.

She could imagine peeling open a tea egg. The cracked brown shell would slide off, wantonly betraying its supple, tan body. She imagined the wafting smell of tea, and the salty taste of soy sauce. Her stomach groaned as she bit down on the egg-white and reached all the way down to the yellow, grainy yolk.

All she could taste in her mouth, however, were paper corn wafers. She wet her lips and swallowed. The train was leaving in ten minutes, leaving the new concrete station. Leaving the stocky man and his tin pot of tea eggs.

She lingered in her seat, then stood up. Her numb legs tingled. So many hours without moving—her aching body reoriented itself.

The other passengers in her car still slept. Quietly, she moved past them, just like she used to tip-toe past her brother's vicious dog in the morning to go to school.

The tea-egg vendor had a crinkly smile and slender hands.

"Get me one from the bottom," she instructed him, watching the pot with big eyes. "They have more flavor at the bottom."

With nimble, stoic fingers, he picked an egg that was fully hidden in the pot. It was marred with a roadmap of cracks.

She handed him a carefully folded five mao from her pocket as he handed her a plastic bag with her tea egg.

She eagerly peeled the shell, switching the hot egg from one hand to the next. She made herself eat the egg one small bite at a time, savoring it meticulously until she finally ate it all. As she returned to her car, she licked her fingers of the tea and soy sauce. She crumbled the plastic bag, stuck it in her pocket, then felt her stomach turn icy.

Her wooden seat was bare. Her soft, cloth bag of indigo was gone, along with the sleeping woman who sat next to her. The train lurched into movement once again—it was fast departing the concrete station. She knitted her sticky fingers together and sat, head bowed. Her cheeks were wet for the rest of the voyage, and the taste of the tea egg was forgotten.

HELMETS AND SUPPOSED OXYGEN

SEAN KAELLNER, 17

BROAD RIPPLE HIGH SCHOOL
INDIANAPOLIS, IN
TEACHER: LOU DEBRUICKER

I have a helmet of popcorn bags on my head so the steam can go somewhere, and I have two fingernails that don't like growing, which I don't mind—so I swamp my daily thoughts with ideas of stories that I have no business involving myself in, and I think that they can end by themselves, but, just so that they get there by the deadline, I push them a little, and they fly off the swing, landing in the mulch feet-first, yet, they can't help it from lying down, face on the ground for a half a minute.

Every second goes by like a snap, crackle, pop, where the pop is quite exciting, but the tired smell of the snap is laughable, not at all tolerable, and we like making fun of it, and the crackle just crackles, and its sounds are indistinguishable from the sounds of midnight's sleeping sighs.

Why I left my hubcap in the ditch off of Interstate 37 is still a mystery to me, and I wonder how it is faring, because it was a long drop from where it freed itself from its bolts and manacles, and it had such a wonderful glimmer, the kind felt but not seen after getting your teeth cleaned.

Maybe the ceiling will not fall on me today, because it has started to look fidgety, and if there is one thing that you have to look out for once you get settled, it is a fidgety ceiling.

A few people like gossiping about my flimsy glasses and my sight behind them, and all I want out of life is to be a storyteller, a firebrand in a smokestack or in a pile of wet logs, leaves, and twigs, and to create smoke signals that say random sets of words like "Yangtze, climb, relationship, Massachusetts Bay Colony, indeed the starfish," and "My God, how we guess the wrong adjectives to say."

So I feel like, in my unstable abode, and with the scent of artificial butter grease in my hair, that a bear or some enormous raccoon must have gotten off with my hubcap and now uses it as a war helmet in the easily heard combat between street rodents, and the fire that sprouts from what we think of as oxygen, is quickly put out or strengthened by the snapping of two, untrimmed fingers, as the hands of the clock, instead of ticking and tocking, crackle and pop like my jaw under a stethoscope.

THAT SPECIAL TIME OF YEAR

GABE LEWIN, 16

HOPEWELL VALLEY CENTRAL HIGH SCHOOL
PENNINGTON, NJ
TEACHER: THERESA SOLOMON

KINDERGARTEN

Thanksgiving ended, and it began. The decorations were strung throughout the classroom and the chatter about gifts and Santa started. I was the only one in my class who didn't celebrate Christmas, so I was the one who ruined the fun for everyone else.

I was the one who had secretly been afraid of Santa. To help me deal with my fear, my mother had long ago told me that Santa Claus isn't real, leaving me in an awkward, confusing situation as everyone else spent the month of December discussing his greatness with unwavering faith. At least I wasn't scared.

Every day, we read books about Christmas. One day, we gathered on the carpet to hear *The Polar Express*, in which a boy gets a bell for Christmas from Santa that only people who believe in Santa can hear ring. While other people hear the bell ring only as a child, the boy still hears it when he's old. When the teacher, Mrs. Thims, was finished reading the book, she whipped out a box of bells from behind her chair, called up each kid, and asked if he or she believed in Santa. After each kid answered with an enthusiastic "Yes," Mrs. Thims replied with, "Then you'll always hear the ring," picked up a bell, rang it, and sent the kid back to the other side of the classroom, bell in hand.

I was called up last, after everyone else had left.

"Do you believe in Santa," she started and upon seeing my hesitation, added, "for other children?" I wanted to say no, but it's hard to stand out at any age, and at five it's even harder.

"Y-Yes."

I've regretted my answer ever since.

FIRST GRADE

The month of December was no longer completely Christmas but had some Hanukkah thrown in too, thanks to the efforts of the principal to modernize the school. The thinking seemed to be, "Because the jews (lowercase) have a holiday around the same time, we'll work it in and everyone'll be happy."

So my meaning-no-harm teacher, Mrs. Yats, tried to teach about Hanukkah and Kwanza too, getting many of the facts wrong in the process. One day she suffered a brief spell of confusion over whether the Maccabees were black or not.

I still stood out. One morning, we went around in a circle and shared with the class something that we were looking forward to over winter vacation. Hanukkah was over, so I couldn't talk about that. Every other kid said some variation of, "I'm looking forward to Christmas, especially the presents."

When my turn came, I mumbled something about New Year's.

THIRD GRADE

My teacher, Mrs. Marks, had everyone make a holiday card for a parent or sibling. Hanukkah had ended the previous week. When I told her this, she suggested I make a New Year's card. I complied, but begrudgingly so. (Who gives out New Year's cards?) I couldn't be too mad, though, because the changes to the school were new, and Mrs. Marks was such a nice teacher who always meant well.

FOURTH, FIFTH, SIXTH, AND SEVENTH GRADE

Teachers no longer obsessed over Christmas. Even in the kindergarten classroom, Mrs. Thims's bell ritual had been halted by the principal, and overall, the Christmas celebration was less intense. Sometimes we still went around the classroom and shared something we were excited about for the holiday season, but by this point, I didn't mumble.

Still, throughout December, and sometimes even November, I remained pale as every other kid was aglow with excitement for Christmas.

EIGHTH GRADE

With the increased demands of the middle school curriculum, teachers didn't have the time to start their Christmas celebrations in school.

But in eighth grade, they found the time. Two days before winter break, the teachers cancelled official classes and had us gather in the library to do special "holiday" activities. In the afternoon, they gathered construction paper and markers and told us to create "a Christmas or whatever holiday you celebrate" card. It would be graded and count as a small quiz in science class. Hanukkah had ended, and when I informed one of the teachers of this, she told me to make something and save it for next year. I wasn't sure if she was serious; after realizing that she was, I walked away grimacing.

Between the stacks of red and green construction paper and markers, I managed to find a lone sheet of white printer paper and a blue marker (Israeli colors, so automatically Hanukkah colors too). I wasn't going to bother stashing some pointless Hanukkah card in my basement for next year, so I hastily put together a Hanukkah card for my dad, putting little effort into it with the plan of throwing it away at the first possible moment.

When it was graded, points were taken off for lack of effort. My science grade suffered.

At the end of the day, the vice principal announced that the draconian school rule against hat-wearing would not be in effect the next day so that students could wear their Santa hats.

After bemoaning this to my parents that night, my dad joked that

I wear a yarmulke. This seemed a bit radical, so I settled on my beloved Chicago Cubs hat to be my headpiece of defiance, an odd choice considering their previous 90-some straight seasons of embarrassment. That night I stashed it in an unused pocket of my backpack with the plan of putting it on once I got to school. Finally, I was going to rebel.

I never had the courage to open the pocket.

TIME IN TERMS OF NATURE

MAXINE MCGREDY, 13

HUNTER COLLEGE HIGH SCHOOL
NEW YORK, NY
TEACHER: LOIS REFKIN

I walk, bundled in a winter coat
On this blustery December day,
Staring at the pavement, waiting
To see my favorite tree.
I've named it Delilah, and so it stands
In front of the house of my dreams.
A perfect circle, Delilah is,
But, alas, she is not perfect.
Someone has tattooed her,
Against her will,
Of course,
With a proclamation of love:
A and K forever.
The words are written in orange ink,
In loopy, orange scrawl,
As though they forgot that the
Being they wrote upon
Was living as well.
The grass beside me
Is brown, not green,
Withered and forlorn,
And the canopy of branches above
Embrace, just like the shadows.

The tree opposite Delilah
Is the tallest I've ever seen,
Reaching far above the rooftops,
And into the azure sky.
A flash of red
Obscures my vision,
And a whisper of wings as well.
The cardinal zips away,
Leaving me
Speechless.
The maroon monster backs into its
Parking spot,
The bully in his seat,
The unwritten rule that must be followed.
The chestnut tree approaches,
It's branches extended,
The warm brown nuts
Hidden in the grass.
I see the robin perch itself atop the maroon car,
And the bluebird swoops in,
Quickly darting away.
The bushes in back
Have become red and black in spots,
The leaves little lemons,
Falling gently to the earth.
And finally, I near the end of my journey,
Near the streetcurb,
Where, in the same orange handwriting,
Someone has written across the road,
"Here we parted."

BIRTHRIGHT
ALLEN BUTT, 17
SOUTH CAROLINA GOVERNOR'S SCHOOL FOR THE ARTS
  AND HUMANITIES
GREENVILLE, SC
TEACHER: GEORGE SINGLETON

A while after my mother disappeared, my father devoted himself to science. This was part of his strategy of exploring, rather than experiencing, grief. But he didn't know much about it and came up with insane, pseudoscientific ideas better suited to a medieval alchemist's lab than to our home, which was caught between woods and early-'90s suburbs in the South. When, after four years, my mother had not returned, he decided she must have died, and he became obsessed with his theory of reincarnation. He tried to explain this to me.

"Richard, look at it this way," he said. "It's not that when we die we return as another being. Our essence is absorbed by what is most important to us." This was how my father always talked. He didn't have much formal education, and nothing seemed to scare him more than the idea that people might assume he was unintelligent. To drive the point home, he wasted no opportunity to show off the vocabulary he'd picked up just by reading the newspaper every morning. "My lexicon has not suffered for my education," he would often say.

At 11, his idea made no sense to me. At 23, it still seems silly, but I can see the logic in it. Even more than that, I can guess why it was so important to him. If my mother had died, then whoever was closest to her would have taken on her characteristics—and, if he could find some of her in himself, that would mean she died caring for him. I think this is what he was driving at.

Still, it struck me as nonsense. I was 11, and I went to a Baptist school (my mother's doing); new ideas of spirituality were beyond my concern. "I don't understand," I told him.

He said that was okay, I didn't have to understand. "I'll prove it to you," he said, excited, I thought, by his own ingenuity, "with science!"

Standing with my father in the pet store, I could smell the animals' food, wood shavings, and the stale scent of urine wafting from open cages. "Do we have to stay here?" I asked him. I hated the place. I thought the animals stared when I turned my back.

"Only long enough to pick out a couple rabbits," he said.

An employee approached us. "Can I help you?" she said.

"Those rabbits," my father said, pointing. "Do they like each other?" She asked what he meant. "Are they solitary, or will they bond?"

"I guess they'll bond."

"About how much food do they need?"

She ran down the list of procedures. Pellets, water, lettuce. At my age, I wondered why she didn't say anything about carrots.

"And what would happen if I didn't feed them?" She looked confused, so he clarified himself. "How long would they take to starve?"

"A couple weeks," she said, then composed herself. "But, sir, I can't sell you an animal if you're not going to care for it."

My father laughed. "Just a joke," he said and bought two.

"What should we call them?" my father asked as we drove home with the rabbits.

"I don't know," I said. I wanted nothing to do with this. Ever since my mother disappeared, I'd put up with his increasingly erratic behavior. If we weren't sitting in the woods trying to hear what the trees had to say, we were playing chess without pieces (to strengthen our memories) or looking for acrostic messages in *The Beaufort Gazette*. I was just becoming old enough to resent him.

"Well, at least come up with something!" he said. "Come on, I'm trying to get you to be useful. That's a real virtue in life."

I figured I'd do what he wanted, so he'd stop nagging me. "Call them Jacob and Esau."

"That's a great idea," he said. "You really don't know what good names those are for these rabbits. I'm very pleased with your creativity." He was quiet for a little while, then said, "You know, your mother would be proud."

I turned away from him, toward the window.

My father's idea?—starve Esau. The name I'd chosen, he told me, was a bit of unintentional gallows humor. Since the famous Esau had sold his birthright for food, our Esau would die for lack of it.

"You're going to kill a rabbit?"

"No, Richard. I'm going to sacrifice it. For science."

"Please don't kill the rabbit."

"Don't cry. You'll scare Jacob and Esau."

He explained to me that this was the best way to objectively test his theory of reincarnation. He would continue feeding Jacob as was considered appropriate for a rabbit. Then, when Esau died, he would allow Jacob to eat as much as he wanted. If Jacob developed a ravenous appetite, we'd know he had absorbed Esau's soul.

"Do rabbits have souls?" I asked.

"Don't ask stupid questions," my father said. "I'm trying to teach you about the natural world. There are people who get paid a lot of money to come up with ideas as good as this one. And sometimes, for the sake of progress, animals have to give their souls to science. This is collectivity. Us and the animals—we're in this together."

When my father fed Jacob, he would take Esau out of the cage and put him on the living room floor, so I could play with him. At first, he would jump around, a little afraid of me, but fairly active nonetheless. After a week, though, he wasn't doing so well. He'd walk tentatively across the floor, and he usually tried to stay close to a wall or the furniture. I watched him sniff around, probably looking for food. I even considered feeding him, but I knew my father would keep an eye out for mutiny. In matters of science, as in those concerning my mother, I was expected to defer to him.

"Richard, are you taking notes?" my father asked me. "You should really consider keeping a diary about this. I would if I was any good at writing. If people start to really believe in reincarnation, we'll be remembered as scientific trailblazers. A diary might be worth a lot one day. It would be like the inheritance I could never give you."

I tried to tune him out and play with Esau. I decided if the rabbit tried to bite me, I wouldn't defend myself. It was hungry and needed my flesh more than I did.

I changed the topic. "I'm really sore," I told my father.

"Well, have you done anything strenuous?"

"No."

"Maybe you're having a growth spurt," he said. "Man, I really do wish I had time to write a diary about this. Something whiz-bang and exciting. But you know I am a slave to my responsibility. I don't have time to spend frivolously; it's all I can do to find time for Jacob and Esau and science. If I had the opportunity today for an education like yours, I wouldn't squander it."

My fifth grade teacher said I didn't seem my usual self. "Are you sick?" she asked. "Because you can go home if you're sick."

"No," I said. "I don't want to go home. My dad's rabbit is dying." This didn't seem to satisfy her, so I added, "Also, I'm having a growth spurt."

She gave back our most recent religion tests. I'd nearly failed, because I couldn't keep Elijah and Elisha straight. There I was at the top of the paper: Richard Murray, Jr., 75 percent. My father was a very tall man. When I got a low grade, I tried to appreciate the duality— that I was, for now, only three fourths of him. But I would have to dispose of this paper before going home. After class, I went to the dumpster behind the school, balled up the paper with my name, and threw it away.

Then Esau died. I wasn't surprised, but I was still a little upset—I'd never been party to something's death before. My father spent every spare moment that week watching Jacob. Jacob didn't seem to eat any more than usual. But, unfortunately, I'd been very hungry that week, probably because of the growth spurt. I'd spent nearly as much time with Esau as Jacob had—if I ate a lot, I knew what my father would think. I decided I was going to have to fast.

"Don't you want something to eat?" he asked me that night at the table. I shook my head. He looked concerned. "Are you sure?" I nodded. He pondered it for a moment, then said, "Did watching Esau die hurt your appetite?" I shrugged. "Well you know, Richard," he said, "sometimes things die, and it isn't anybody's fault."

My fast did cause trouble at school. Two days in, as I handed in my homework, my teacher asked me why I was so sluggish. I told her I hadn't slept well the night before.

"Did you forget to say your prayers?" she asked.

"Probably," I said.

The homework had been to write one paragraph on any Biblical event. I chose God's gift of manna and pheasants to the Israelites when they wandered in the desert. Manna and pheasants was a really good present to give hungry people, I had written, which is why Moses was punished when he struck the stone for water. He was only supposed to ask permission, but that wasn't good enough for Moses. No way! He just had to smack it, so then he couldn't go into the Promised Land of Milk and Honey, and, if I had been an Israelite, I wouldn't have let him eat any of my pheasants.

I didn't get a spectacular grade for that assignment either.

I broke my fast after four days. By that time, I was so hungry that I ate all the food my father made for dinner, and I still wanted more. My father was pleased.

"I knew it!" he said. "You played with Esau so much, you were more important to him than Jacob. Took a while, though—I guess there's a latency period." Then he got excited. "You know what this means, right, Richard? We're going to be world-famous scientists."

He spent most of the night pondering his discoveries. He didn't talk about it again until that Saturday, when he told me he was going to the public library to research "past advances in the science of reincarnation."

"Also," he said, "I've been thinking about the results and their implications for our situation. Since I don't seem to have become any more like your mother used to be, and neither have you, then if she died, she must have died happy. Really something to think about, huh?" Then he left.

I was furious. I had never been furious before—when my mother disappeared, I was too young to really grasp the idea of fury. But I was just old enough at 11 to understand that he'd starved the rabbit over her. Even then, I knew she wasn't coming back, whether she was dead or not. I didn't know why she left, and I didn't expect to learn; it was enough to know she was gone. I decided something had to be done.

Without any reminders of my mother, I thought, my father might have a better chance of forgetting about her. So I gathered all the photographs of her in the house, and I cut them into long strips with a pair of scissors. By the time I was done, I had what looked like a pile of glossy confetti on the floor, which I swept into the trash.

"So, why'd you do it?"
"I don't know."
"You know, she's your mother. Not just my wife."
"I know."

"Your mother."

I think my father was too exhausted to be angry. But I could tell he was upset that he didn't have the pictures anymore. Which was why he started taking art classes at the community college—so he could draw her picture before the memory faded.

"We start off just drawing with pens and pencils," he told me, "but if we master that pretty fast, we might move on to charcoal and paint before too long."

"Charcoal, huh?"

"You know," he said, "I always thought charcoal was just for barbecue, but apparently it's also used for making art."

"That's really interesting, Dad."

"I know, isn't it? Also," and his eyes sparkled at this, "this is a little controversial in a small town of this nature, but, if our class shows especially high potential, we may work with nude models." Then he started laughing, and I realized he was joking, trying to ease the tension between us. I snickered a little, to appease him.

I played on the floor with Jacob while my father sketched at the kitchen table. Jacob hopped around, occasionally approaching me, but more often checking out the room for himself. He hadn't spent nearly as much time outside the cage as Esau had—but that seemed to me a fair trade-off for continued life. At the moment, he was sniffing one of the legs of the table.

"How's that rabbit doing?" my father asked.

"He's okay," I said. "I don't like him as much as Esau."

"That's because Esau was selfless, Richard. He knew what he had to do, and he did it. Jacob's lived a comparably sheltered life." He said he had to use the bathroom and stood up and left. While he was gone, I looked at the picture he was drawing.

On the page, shaky lines made a deformed circle of a head, with little ovals for eyes and a lopsided mouth. Still, I could tell it was my mother represented by the thin lines of lead on paper—my mother as I might have seen her had I just awoken some afternoon, my eyes not yet adjusted to the light.

When my father came back to the room, I said, "Dad, I'm sorry I ruined all the pictures of Mom."

He looked at me, completely quiet, his eyes blank, and nodded to himself. Then he sat back down to the table and continued putting the final touches on his picture.

"I'm not going to take any more art classes," he told me. "It's too expensive. And I've already gotten what I wanted out of it."

The next day at school, we had our weekly art class. Our regular teacher took us to the art teacher's room, and we stayed there for 45 minutes, learning to draw scenes from the Bible. The teacher often praised my patience and my ability to draw mostly straight lines in crayon.

"What Bible story would you like to draw today?" she asked us.

"Jacob and Esau," I said, before anyone in class could pre-empt me.

"That's not a very interesting story," she said. "Wouldn't you rather do Jacob wrestling with the angel?"

"No," I said. "Jacob and Esau."

"All right, Jacob and Esau," she said. "Let's see what we can do with this."

She turned to the blackboard and drew Esau—a man with long, shaggy hair, dressed in animal fur—standing in the foreground facing backward. In the background, facing Esau, she drew Jacob, fair skinned, clean shaven, stirring a pot on what looked like an electric stove. I thought of Esau saying, "Behold, I am at the point to die: and what profit shall this birthright do to me?" and I thought of Jacob, later, kneeling before his blind father in deception. I thought of their mother, Rebekah, how she must have internalized over so many years that the elder would serve the younger. And I thought of their father, Isaac, tied to a pyre, as his own father raised a sacrificial knife.

"All right, class," our teacher said when she was done. "See if you can draw that."

I looked at the picture. It was simple, and it was uninteresting. But I knew, looking at it, I could not possibly draw Jacob and Esau any way the class might comprehend. Still, this was class—I had to do something. I lifted my pencil. I held it to the page, and I began to draw. I tried not to think of my father. I tried not to think of my mother, maybe reincarnated in my pencil's graphite tube, the image I created, or the sequence that had led me to create it.

SESAME STREET WHEN THE CAMERA'S OFF

AIDAN GRAHAM, 12

WILLIAM ALEXANDER MIDDLE SCHOOL
BROOKLYN, NY
TEACHER: JOHN MCENENY

PLOT SYNOPSIS

Cookie Monster is a character on the long-running popular children's program *Sesame Street*, with other Muppets such as Elmo, Oscar the Grouch, and Big Bird. The show's Director, Stan Speilburg, gets a letter from the Vice President of Shut Down T.V. Shows Because They Make Our Children Fat Company and mother of a child viewer who watches *Sesame Street*. Her child, Chubby Simon-Simmons, has grown fat because he eats too many cookies. His Australian mother, Sydney Simon-Simmons, the Soccer Mom and Vice President of SDTVSBTMOCFC, believes that Cookie Monster is at fault for her child's obesity so she strongly requests that he be fired immediately. Stan Speilburg, the Director, adhering to the child's mother, fires Cookie Monster. Chaos ensues. A new monster is hired who is sneaky and untrustworthy. In the back of this new monster's mind is the eventual takeover of *Sesame Street*. When the show's cast starts to break away, only Oscar is left alone. With the help of Sydney the Soccer Mom, who has had a recent change of heart about Cookie Monster, he tries to get Cookie Monster to return to the show and street. Yet Cookie Monster has other big plans for his life after writing an exposé about himself in his autobiographical book titled *No Moping for This Muppet*. This time, the cast of *Sesame Street* splits up for good.

CHARACTER SYNOPSIS

COOKIE MONSTER

Cookie Monster is the protagonist in this story. He is a large blue ravenous monster who used to have a passion for cookies only to change his mind by eating only vegetables when he became too fat and lost his girlfriend, Candy Lake. He is obsessed with self-image and becomes very narcissistic. He would love for things to have stayed the way they were on *Sesame Street* but is jolted into reality when losing his job after being confronted by the Director, who received negative threats by an unhappy viewer who accuses Cookie Monster of helping her son become obese. When Cookie Monster is finally acquitted of any wrongdoing, he does not return to *Sesame Street* but moves on—writing his autobiography and becoming a best-selling author.

VEGGIE MONSTER

Veggie Monster is the antagonist in this story. He is a five-foot-eleven-inch tall green monster who has green brussel sprout eyes, an onion nose, red-bell-pepper lips, and spaghetti squash hair. He is sneaky and untrustworthy. He wants to get Cookie Monster off of *Sesame Street* and will do everything in his power to do this. He is threatening to the other monsters on the street and comes off as a big-time bully. When eventually found out to be the monster that he is, he slinks away into obscurity.

DIRECTOR – (MR. STAN SPEILBURG)

Director is the man in charge of the *Sesame Street* production. He is not a monster but a human being. He is a slight man who wears dark black round glasses and dark suits. He is easily manipulated and afraid to be found out as the woman that he is. He is not strong in spirit and immediately wants Cookie fired when confronted by an angry soccer mom even though Cookie Monster has been with the show for over 37 years. He is a man who has no loyalty.

Sydney Simon-Simmons – The Soccer Mom
(Must have Australian accent)

Sydney the Soccer Mom is the Vice President of Shut Down T.V. Shows Because They Make Our Children Fat Company from Australia and mother of Chubby Simon-Simmons, her nine-year-old son. Sydney the Soccer Mom is an obnoxious yuppie-type woman who is extremely pushy and demanding. She is a large woman who generally gets her way with everything she wants. When demanding that Cookie Monster be fired because of her son's personal issues, the Director caves in immediately and causes a whole change of life for the *Sesame Street* community.

Elmo

Elmo is a furry red Muppet with a seedy past. He used to be the leading character on *Sesame Street* but struggled with being found out for who he truly was—a former Bloods gang member. Although he insists that he was pulled into the Bloods because of the color of his fur, he was constantly frightened that the newspaper rags would out him. Even though he was Cookie Monster's very good friend, he stopped fighting for him when Veggie Monster threatened him with his job.

Oscar the Grouch

Oscar is the Grouch monster who struggles with being Happy. He has been in therapy for this Happy behavior for a long time and works hard at trying to figure out who he really is on a daily basis. He lived in a garbage can next to the 123 Sesame Street Apartment Building all the while he lived in Sesame Street but was evicted when his can went condo because of the change in the Street. He was the monster who—with Sydney the Soccer Mom—tried to talk Cookie Monster to come back to *Sesame Street* to no avail.

Oprah Winfrey

Oprah Winfrey is another human character in the story. She is the owner, writer, producer, director, and star of *The Oprah Winfrey Show*. She is also a person who interviews Cookie Monster on her show and is about to catapult Cookie Monster into greatness by advertising his autobiographical book—*No Moping for This Muppet*—on her daily television show and making the book the next Oprah Book Club Selection.

■

ACT I, SCENE FOUR

Elmo and Cookie Monster are finishing up a scene on the set of Sesame Street. *Veggie Monster approaches. Director is sheepishly standing behind Veggie Monster.*

On air, facing camera and smiling

Elmo: *(Holding up a red Elmo doll)* . . . And that, boys and girls . . . is why you should never eat red things. If you eat red things, your face will turn red, your hands will turn red, your legs will turn red, your whole body will turn red. And if you turn red, you can't go to bed because you'll probably be dead.

Director: Cut t t t. That's a wrap . . .

Veggie Monster: Well then.

Elmo: Who is the green guy?

Veggie Monster: I am Cookie Monster's replacement.

Elmo: Oh my gosh . . . I did not see Cookie getting fired coming this way! Cookie being fired is outrageous. He is my best and dearest friend. I would do anything for him. He does not eat red things! He is a loyal member of our *Sesame Street* community. I protest!

Veggie Monster: You better be quiet because it could be you going off the street. *(Elmo quickly becomes silent.)* Alright let's just film the next scene.

Elmo, Veggie Monster and Cookie Monster sit next to each other smiling.

Cookie Monster: *(Turns to Veggie Monster)* What's up? You're new here, huh? I like the color of your fur.

Veggie Monster: So do I.

Cookie Monster: Is it natural or dyed?

Veggie Monster: Everything about me is fake . . . I mean dyed.

Cookie Monster: I am beginning to notice some gray hairs in my fur now. So I probably will soon have to start dying it too. When you have been on the air as long as I have, you have to keep up the good looks.

Director: And . . . Action!

Cookie Monster: *(Talking to Veggie Monster)* Wait. Who are you?

Veggie Monster: Good morning folks! Today we have a very sad day in *Sesame Street* history.

Cookie Monster: *(Very confused, looking around)* Whoa . . . What's going on here? Those words are not on the cue cards!

Veggie Monster: *(Looking at camera)* Today, Cookie Monster will be leaving the *Sesame Street* community.

Cookie Monster: (*Jumping out of his seat raising his arms in disbelief and pulling out his fur. He begins angrily pacing back and forth behind Veggie, who is still calm and collected in his seat.*) What is happening! I cannot be getting fired! I am a television icon!

Veggie Monster: (*Looking to the camera*) We all agreed that you leaving *Sesame Street* would be for the best.

Cookie Monster: When did I agree to leave?!!

Veggie Monster: (*To camera*) Cookie Monster will not be returning to the show next week. Instead he will be replaced with me, Veggie Monster. The letter C is for Cookies. Cookies are for Criminals. The letter V is for Veggies. Veggies are for Valedictorians. See you next time. (*Holding up his two fingers in the form of a V*).

Director: Annnd Cut!

Cookie Monster: I can't believe this is happening. I eat veggies too! I am better than you. You can't handle this job! You are fake and phony. You dye your fur! You have to be real to be on *Sesame Street* . . . you . . . . you . . . you . . . you . . . creep.

Veggie Monster: Sticks and stones will break my bones but names—

Cookie Monster: Yeah, stick and stones? Thanks for the information.

Veggie Monster: S is for (*yells*) Securityyy! Oh, and by the way, Cooks, I hear there's a spot on Telly Tubbies. Tinky Winky told me Talking Sun is getting the boot.

Cookie Monster: (*Crying and yelling*) Watch! I'll be back. You'll see. This show is nothing without me. Without me, this show is nothing. In a couple of years Big Bird is going to play for the NBA, and I'm going to go inform *People* magazine of Elmo's former gang days with the Bloods!

Elmo: Oh dear . . . That was many years ago . . . and I was forced to join because I was red! You cannot bring my past into your mess. No one brings up that Big Bird was a Latin King.

Cookie Monster: Yeah and then I'm going to tell everyone that Oscar the Grouch is not a Grouch at all and that Big Bird wears lifts in his claws and that Mr. Speilburg is really Miss Speilburg. I'm not done with you. All of you . . . be afraid . . . be very afraid! *(Cookie Monster exits angrily)*

Elmo: Should I be afraid?

Veggie Monster: . . . no.

■

ACT II, SCENE SEVEN
Cookie Monster appears on The Oprah Winfrey Show, *where Oprah wants to discuss Cookie's life and his new autobiography* No Moping for This Muppet.

Oprah: *(To audience)* Good afternoon, everyone, my name is Oprah Winfrey and I am the owner, writer, producer, director and star of *The Oprah Winfrey Show*. I am also the person who could make any writer's dream come true because just my mentioning their book on my show could catapult them to greatness and get them lots and lots of dough— as in money not cookie dough. So let me introduce you to the man of the hour. The man, or should I say monster . . . who did it all . . . from his days on *Sesame Street* to his days on the mean streets of *Law and Order—Special Victims Unit* . . . To his becoming a world-renowned author writing his autobiography . . . Meet the author of our next Oprah Book Club Selection . . . Mr. Cookie Monsterrrr!—talking about his gripping life in the book *No Moping for This Muppet*!!!

Enter Cookie Monster waving to audience

Cookie Monster: Good morning, Oprah! I am honored that you asked me to be on your show. This yellow couch is even comfier than it looks on television. I almost feel like jumping on it.

Oprah: My pleasure. So Cookie, tell us about your new book! It's been on the *New York Times* Best Seller List for the past six months.

Cookie Monster: My new autobiography, *No Moping for This Muppet* covers everything! My abusive childhood, my favorite cookie recipes, my wild and fast-paced days on *Sesame Street*, the whole Veggie Monster scandal, and, of course, my weight struggle. You must know about that Oprah. I was finally comfortable enough to share with the world my life on the street uncovered. Nothing is hidden.

Oprah: Girlfriend . . . do I understand weight struggles. It is no wonder that this wonderful book is on the best-sellers list! So we hear that *Sesame Street* is done and that it has been replaced by that little girl with brown hair—Dora the Explorer. What can you tell us about all of your old friends and what's happening in their lives.

Cookie Monster: Sadly, we decided as a group that *Sesame Street* had run its course . . . The monsters didn't seem like monsters anymore . . . they were becoming so much more human-like, with human problems and tribulations. You know how humans are . . . They are not that much fun. In fact, they are pretty boring. And more importantly . . . humans cannot act!

Oprah: I see . . .

Cookie Monster: Yes. Even Count is working as an accountant in a law firm. Can't get any more ugly human than working in a law firm.

Oprah: Wow! Imagine.

Cookie Monster: Yes. We all still keep in touch, but kids these days are more into Spongebob Circle Pants and North Park than watching me eat cookies and Elmo singing the alphabet incorrectly.

Oprah: Now we have a commercial break, but when we come back Cookie Monster shares with us the drama of being a detective on *Law and Order: Special Victims Unit* and how he went from being fired to being one of the most powerful men in the world!

Cookie Monster: Technically . . . monster.

PH.D.
SARAH CARNICK, 18
SOUTH CAROLINA GOVERNOR'S SCHOOL FOR THE ARTS
  AND HUMANITIES
GREENVILLE, SC
TEACHER: MAIME MORGAN

I'm writing a book, a breakthrough
in human analysis, entire chapters
devoted to how a day feels,
what it is to mistake Thursday
for a Tuesday.

There is an index in the back
organized by quality.

It starts with what makes
the least sense (Congress)
and ends with what makes
the most (my mother's smile).

I write about the essence
of why man is different,
but I haven't mentioned a thing
about opposable thumbs—the way they close
a man's mind and body
around the handle of an ax.

I name symptoms once considered
anatomically necessary—
this is me calling out the appendix

and asking it some crucial questions.
Why are you here? Did people look
too silly with a concave side?
Are you some kind of filler,
like a bad line in a decent song?

I'm walking through doors
no one ever noticed before
and making it all up
as I go along.

CARAMEL
MATTHEW JOSEPH DISLER, 13
COLLEGIATE SCHOOL
RICHMOND, VA
TEACHER: KATE CUNNINGHAM

Winterville Road was at the very end of town, in an ancient area filled with musty Victorian homes. However, the house at the end of Winterville Road could not be called Victorian, unlike its neat, gabled neighbors. It was a pudgy, squat thing, with stones haphazardly piled on top of one another to form lopsided walls. The roof was made of weather-beaten, thatched tiles, and a large maple tree grew in front of the door.

An old lady lived in that house, and every day after school, my friends and I would canter up to her residence and draw straws to see who would have to knock on the door. Then, one of us would creep up the moldy front steps and gently rap on the great, oversized eagle-headed brass knocker on the door. The old woman would open the door promptly, her puckered-up face eyeing us warily.

I can't imagine that she ever enjoyed our visits, for her countenance, when she opened the door, was always begrudging. She must have hated us and the annoying disturbance we created in her life. My friends and I didn't even like her that much. It was her candies we came for, because she always had a large cauldron of melted caramel bubbling on her hearth. We asked for spoonfuls when we knocked on her door.

"Please, Miss," we would say, as the sweet, sugary smell of the candy wafted out of the doorway, "are you making any caramels today?"

And, reluctantly, she would open the door a little wider and beckon us in. She never talked when we came for candy, and even when we had entered her house, she would eye us suspiciously, with a grimace on her face.

There were always five of us who came for candy: Herman, David,

Frank, Philip, and me. And, curiously, there were always five ladles in the cauldron. I think she expected our visits, and though our daily expeditions to her house may have become routine, they did not improve her disposition. She would glare at us one by one as we tentatively approached the cauldron, grasped a ladle, and sipped daintily at the liquid candy. Herman always sipped caramel first, and then Frank, Philip, David, and I followed. I remember the taste of that caramel. I could feel the sugar dancing on my tongue, and then the caramel would glide down my throat, warming every square inch of my esophagus like a daily dose of cocoa.

But the old lady at the end of Winterville Road never shared in our sampling when we were with her. As soon as we each had our turns she would swiftly usher us back through the entrance and slam the door. We would not see her again until the next day.

She never talked to us, she never smiled at us, and never came out of her house.

Ever.

It was hard to guess who could have known her well enough to have left that baby girl on her front steps.

I remember the day when the baby came. It was November 11th, 1950, and the first snow of the season had fallen the previous night. A thin, pearly layer of the stuff covered everything, like a wool blanket for the whole world.

My companions and I scampered off to the end of Winterville Road as soon as school let out, pulling on our hats and yanking on our gloves as we ran. Our breath came out in little fluctuating clouds, and we occasionally stopped at roadside snowdrifts for little snowball fights. But soon our shoes got wet from the snow, and cold water began to seep through the soles. Recalling our mothers' warnings about catching a cold, we hurried off to the house at the end of Winterville Road.

We arrived, panting, in front of the old woman's home. Huddling under the maple tree, we waited impatiently as Herman took out his straws.

"Come on," Frank whined. "I'm freezing!"

"Wait a second, will ya?" Herman snapped back, rummaging in his jacket. "I know they're in here somewhere, and it's only a matter of time before I—here they are!"

His gloved hands pulled out the straws. He had swiped them from a restaurant three years ago, and he kept them wherever he went. There was always a short one; whoever picked it was forced to knock on the old woman's door.

We each plucked a straw from his outstretched hand, and then viewed our comparative sizes. Soon a mournful cry arose from Philip.

"Shoot! I got the short straw one yesterday!"

"Tough," said Herman.

"Yeah," said David, Herman's little brother. "Tough!" He giggled a little bit, snorted, and then fell silent.

"Come on," I said in my prepubescent, quiet voice, "just go."

"All right, but if I get the short straw tomorrow, I'm not doing it!" retorted Philip.

"Hurry up. I'm cold," Frank repeated. Philip gave him a contemptuous glance. Then, hesitantly as always, he crept up to the front door and rapped on the door with the eagle-head knocker.

Nothing happened.

"Is she dead?" asked Frank, surprised.

"Shut up, you idiot!" admonished Herman. "She might be listening!"

And we waited silently, not daring to breathe, lest karma cause her to keep the door closed. A northerly wind rustled the branches of the oak tree and pricked our insides with a frigid caress. A dog barked, and I could hear a radio playing Doris Day's "Bewitched" in the distance.

Then the door swung open. There was the old woman, looking haggard and tired. Her gray hair, normally in a tight bun, fell about her head in clumps, and faded plaid pajamas hung about her bony frame. Her unusually watery blue eyes quickly took us all in, and she frowned, her lower lip trembling.

"No caramel today!" she cried out to us. A baby began wailing, and her head snapped back behind her. A letter in her hand dropped to the floor as she let out a soft sob, and she quickly slammed the door shut.

Philip turned around, and we looked at each other, amazed.

"She talked," he gasped.

We wandered back up Winterville Road, dazed, and we gradually found our way back to our respective houses. As usual, while returning home, I said nothing, for I was always the shy one in our little group. I rarely spoke, and I usually tagged behind Herman with David, but I was exceptional in one sense: I was the fastest runner in town. I mostly used my speed in races on the way to the old woman's house, but I could even outrun Boris Menkievich, who boasted that he had once sprinted past a train.

We didn't go back to the house at the end of Winterfield Road that whole week: we were too bewildered by the old woman's words. I had no chances to race for a while. We merely spent the afternoons meandering about the town, discussing what could have prompted her to speak. David repeatedly asserted that she was possessed by a demon, but nobody ever listened to his superstitious tirades. However, as we strolled along Main Street to Blumenfelds' General Store on Wednesday, Herman remembered the infant voice that had emanated from the house.

"Didn't anybody else hear it?" he asked.

"Hear what?" replied Frank, and Philip cocked his head in bemusement.

"There was a baby crying in the background."

"Shut up, Herman," said Frank, "you must be hearing things."

"Come on," Herman said. "You all know I got the best ears of us"—David grudgingly nodded his head in agreement—"I'm telling you, there was a baby in that house."

But Frank, Philip, and David didn't believe him. They shook their heads and continued to walk down the street. I could hear someone shouting as we passed Brennmun's House of Diamonds, but as I stopped to look in the storefront window, a flurry of snow hurtled in front of my field of vision, heralding an approaching blizzard. Snowstorms had frequented our town in the past week, submerging the rooftops in a thick, powdery blanket.

I looked back at Herman. His eyes were downcast, and his lower lip protruded as he pouted. His feet shuffled in the snow, making long, ditch-like tracks behind them. Feeling sorry for him, I decided to take action.

"I heard it too."

They all turned to look at me. David contemptuously turned around and began striding to the general store, which was now in sight, but he turned back once he realized that the others were standing still. He walked back to us as a figure covered in scarves and shawls pushed a stroller across the street from us, whistling an indistinguishable tune. I shuffled my feet and looked at the ground now that so many eyes were directed toward me.

"Huh," grunted Philip. Nobody talked for a second, as a particularly strong gust of wind made the figure across the street stop and pull its shawls tighter against itself. Then, after their silence, my friends exploded in congratulations to Herman, and they began to chat nonchalantly about the possible reasons that the old lady had a baby in her house, quickly dismissing David's idea that she was a witch and was going to eat the child. They seemed to have forgotten me. I followed them in my usual silence as they walked the last few hundred feet to the general store.

I cannot say that their ignorance of me did not hurt. Back then, I often felt a distinct tinge of sadness when I was with my friends, for I seemed insignificant, a mere tool for them to accomplish their desires. But I was talented at overcoming my emotions, and I still wanted my playmates to be with me, despite their disinterest in regards to me, their soft-spoken companion since kindergarten.

Across the street, the shawl-covered creature prepared to traverse the intersection. It pulled its apparel about it one more time, and then began pushing the stroller as a not-too-distant honk sounded. The figure turned its head in surprise, lost its balance on a patch of ice, and fell upon the curb of the sidewalk. The stroller rolled out into the middle of the street. The fallen creature let out a startled yelp, as it landed on its buttocks and its shawls slipped off to reveal the old woman from Winterville Road. Herman's head snapped to stare at her, and the others followed his gaze.

Philip whispered to Frank, "It's her."

The baby started crying at the same time I saw the truck's headlights and heard its engine bellowing, carrying the vehicle far above the speed limit.

SHEOL
PAULA ALBANEZE, 16
MOANALUA HIGH
HONOLULU, HI
TEACHER: LIANE VOSS

The man's eyes cracked open, but the darkness that met them was thicker than the insides of his eyelids. Silence, like a vacuum, further blackened the surroundings into nothing. Heavy breathing escaped his lips, a sound that deserved an echo, but, like everything else, was swallowed up in the immense sea of eternal night. The man waved his hand in front of his face but failed to make out any shape, failed even to notice its movement in the nerves under his skin, or the light breeze it should have made against his face.

Where am I?

Words became trapped in his throat, drowned by the sea of black. Where they clung, his breath would not pass. There was no ground beneath his feet, or else—if there was indeed a surface there—its sturdiness could not be felt by the man's dead nerves. He had the sensation of being deep underwater; no movement, no light, no air; just the vast ocean of blackness, just the void. A hollow pain whistled in his chest as though something that had existed there his entire life was now absent. This feeling of emptiness existed alone in the black sea; there was no other emotion.

Something is missing.

He felt a familiar presence—a breath, perhaps—on his shoulder. The phantom whispered past him, disappearing somewhere in front of the man. In an instant it was a thousand miles away, then it whipped back to face the man in the darkness, its unseen eyes creating a painful itch where they passed over his skin. The itch and the emptiness were all he could feel. A thunderous voice whispered to him, its distance impossible to tell. All at once, it was miles away and echoed within the man's ears as though it originated from within his own head.

"Welcome, child."

The man's spine contorted and his muscles shook at the sound. Father?

"No, I'm afraid not. I have been expecting you for quite some time."

Who are you?

"Be still, child. Do not ask such questions."

I can't see you.

"Yes, do forgive me." Approximately six feet away from the man, a white porcelain mask appeared like a cloud shying away from the bright, milky moon. It was carved as a beautiful maiden, her lips slightly parted in innocent surprise, the white of her glowing face all that could be seen in the black.

I must be dreaming.

The white mask stood perfectly still. "I assure you, you are not."

What is this place?

"This is . . ." A hideous scratching sound, like static, erupted inside the man's ears. It took hold of his brain, drawing little bits of it out, out into the black sea to be washed away with all other senses. The mask's voice faded back in, hideously low and warped with the disturbance. As it spoke, its voice shifted back to its normal tone. "Pardon the disruption; you have yet to reach that stage."

Stage?

"The point upon which you realize where you are."

I don't understand. How did I get here?

"Through a series of misguided choices you wound up where you are now."

Something is missing.

"Do you remember your wife, Lily? Do you remember what she told you every night, before the two of you lay down to sleep?"

Images of past nights flooded the man's thoughts. A green office lamp, a Bible, and a miniature oriental rug adorned the mahogany nightstand beside a bed covered in red and gold fleur-de-lis print. Lily rolled on top of his bare chest, her wavy, auburn hair twisting like birthday ribbons. Dark brown eyes smiled behind thick eyelashes, though her mouth was moving with a muted message of dire urgency. She kissed his lips. Strangely, in his reminiscing, the man felt nothing. Memories that once made him tingle with joy left his heart a vacant hole. The more he thought of his wife, the more she seemed to slip away, sucked into the empty pit in his chest, sinking until there was nothing left of her, not the smile in her eyes nor the ribbons of hair. In moments she was completely forgotten, swept out through his ears and into the empty black sea, torn away on a current too strong to resist.

"Do you remember what she told you?"

The man's head felt washed and weather-beaten.

Who?

"Your wife."

Something else was controlling him. A tangle of veins, a twisting of weeds . . . something struck his hand.

I never married.

A faint, guttural laugh emanated from the mask's direction but was quickly carried away in the motionless, yet powerful ocean. "Do you remember your children?"

A flash of a crooked smile with missing teeth, a blushing child that spoke with his eyes. The man nudged a small rubber ball, yellow with blue stars, towards the infant, who bounced with excitement. An older girl in a white sundress embraced her tiny brother as his arms prepared to grasp the oncoming sphere. The ball hit the boy's foot and rolled off to the man's right. He remembered the feeling of his facial muscles tightening as he pulled up a smile and chased after the ball. The brightly-colored sphere eluded him, turning and spinning faster than he thought possible. The ball darkened, spinning until—like a marble—it shot from his ear and disappeared into the abyss. He turned back toward his children, seeking some sort of steadiness in the familiarity of their faces. Instead, he turned to the dark ink of the ocean, searching for them with his mind. He called out to them, preparing his lips to form their names. Static filled his mind at a deafening volume and all hope of remembrance was dissolved; for whom had he been searching just now? He could not recall. A hollow laugh replaced the white noise and suddenly the mask reappeared before him, a constant presence much like that of a stalking predator.

Why are you doing this?

"You need to learn to let go of your past. I am simply helping you along."

I don't want your help.

"I'm afraid you have no choice."

A sharp pain shot up the man's arm, reverberating in his spine.

"Do you remember your childhood? Your mother and father? Do you remember the time you threw a pool ball at your brother's head?" The mask laughed: a truly disturbing combination of hisses and howls. "You regretted it the moment that eight ball left your fingertips. Do you remember the time you spilled the Communion wine in church? What about the time you kissed your best friend's lover? But most importantly, do you remember taking that extra dose of pills yesterday morning?"

Tingles of pain trickled up the man's spine; this time coming from his fingertips, toes, and even from his eyebrows and cheekbones.

"You emptied a whole bottle; no one survives that."

The pain became stronger, writhing underneath his skin.

My God, what is happening to me?

"God?" The mask shook quickly, revealing for a moment what lay underneath, but it, like everything else, was soon swept out into the nothing and forgotten. "You deserted your God ages ago."

What is going to happen to me?

"My dear child," the thing exclaimed, "it has already happened!"

In a flash of yellow light, the figure behind the mask was illuminated. A frightening thing, alien and horrid in its vague resemblance to a human being, spread to every corner of darkness, occupying the entirety of the ocean. There was no escape for the man's eyes; horror met him at every glance. Dripping, oozing wounds, pulsing organs, skin stretched over a distorted bone structure. The man recoiled in disgust and his eyes fell upon his own naked body.

Thick vines broke through his skin, swimming beneath its surface and stretching further into his organs until they enveloped every bit of him. Blinded by pain, he could barely make out the shapes of other victims within the creature's body, adding to the heaving, perverted mass. Their forms were stretched beyond recognition; their mouths forever open in a static cry as their flesh blended with the creature's. He felt his skin stretch and the vines begin to take control. Before fading into nonexistence, he caught sight of the white mask, forever floating before him in hideous mockery, surveying him with cold, empty eyes.

A, B, C, D, S, E, X

KATIE EISENBERG, 18

CONVENT OF THE SACRED HEART
GREENWICH, CT
TEACHER: MARY LEE RAFFERTY

They say that honesty is the best policy.

They say that truth will set you free.

Yet, as far as I can tell, *they* never had to assess whether or not they had the heart to confess to their parents that they were wholly aware of what the entire reproductive system entailed . . . at the age of six.

It began rather innocently, as most sordid tales do, on one of those rare occasions when my ten-year-old sister and I were dubbed "careful" enough to have the house to ourselves. The parental units were out enjoying a night on the town, which translated to something between "fun!" and "ephemeral rapture" on my personal happiness scale. With the world at my feet, I picked, with stubby fingernails, the lock on the Pandora's Box of the second floor: The Master Bedroom.

I was not one of those impish children who stole her father's shoehorns—that breed of pedestrian behavior was reserved for the amateurs still using sippy cups. I craved something more. *Literature*. My eyes glazed over at the glorious sight of bound leather tomes with gold trims, engraved spines, and bronze tassels, yet, as my passion for the literature of old would not manifest itself for several years, I was sold on the easy winner: The large, cheaply printed picture book with the rainbow on the front cover.

Where Did I Come From? The title screamed in multitonal block print. *Cool,* I mused, *we just learned about immigration in Social Studies.* After scanning the first few pages, I quickly remembered that most people were not cartoonishly bare and entwined as they passed through customs . . . at least, not in our school textbooks. Did I really only have a few years left until the terrors of this strange P-U-B-E-R-T-Y (poo-birdy?) took hold? Was it not, as I had once presumed, possible for one to remain a child forever, in the footsteps of my man-boy hero Peter Pan? *Love is not something one makes,* I scoffed with disgust (though most likely in less eloquent wording), *it is not, like, pudding!* I was horrified, yet my eyes remained glued to the graphically explicit pages. With a sense of urgency that one only sees in the queue for a particularly crowded ladies' room, I skimmed the rest of the disgusting account. Hands shaking, I slid the book back in its place, and proceeded to remove myself from the premises with a trail of dirty, sinful guilt oozing in my wake.

I had undermined one of the holy parental plots, an event which parents take so seriously as to set an exact date and time for the plan of action. I later discovered that their intended procreation revelation would occur just after I opened the gift on my tenth birthday. I feigned surprise about the largest present of all—the knowledge of sexuality, which, regrettably, was not gift-wrapped. Cowardice, of course, has a six-digit price tag on its ugly head, and during the horrible years to follow, I constantly refused to subject myself to the unabridged version of "The Talk" for fear of spilling the proverbial beans all over my new, taffeta party dress.

Of course, as luck (or the cruelty of the Powers That Be) would have it, even the truncated edition of "The Talk" put me at a disadvantage.

During the summer *after* my tenth birthday, my mother finally managed to secure me in the front passenger seat of the old Toyota (with notebooks, hairbrushes, and toys strewn about the back half of the vehicle) after we had pulled into the decrepit parking lot at the Random Farms pool. Oh, she was good—getting me alone in a place where she knew I would never run away, for fear of rabid chipmunks and spoiled, purebred dogs (the pride of the locals) forming an army and foiling my escape plan.

My mother referenced our preliminary discussion in December.

She referenced my health class.

She referenced the school nurse.

She referenced her own "experience" (complete with a teary recollection).

She referenced a series of instructional videos.

She even referenced helpful . . . *books* . . . that she had procured throughout the years.

Overall, it was quite a bit of referencing, and quite a larger bit of crying.

I, turning redder by the second, held my breath, as though letting out a puff of air would suddenly divulge my dirty little secret.

By the time she had finished, the pool had shut down for the night, its gates as stubborn as my disposition at the time.

On the five-minute drive home, I kept myself occupied by pulling the teeth out of a flimsy, fuchsia comb that I had found in the backseat.

Nearly 12 years later, I have yet to retell the horrors of that fateful night to a living soul, and, from time to time, the shame still resurfaces every time I pass the feminine hygiene aisle of the local pharmacy. However, for what it is worth, I have never regretted the transformation brought on by the incident. Granted, perhaps I did not realize it at the time, but this was only the tip of curiosity's iceberg, and being exposed to soft-core pornography in hard-cover form was the blunt ice-pick that chipped away at my shell of immaturity to reveal a newfound adulthood at the chewy center. After all, as the old adage more or less goes, I must know *Where Did I Come From?* to know where I am going.

Which, for all intents and purposes, is not the Master Bedroom.

CIVIL SUCKSTON

STEVEN NIEDBALA, 16

WAYNESBURG CENTRAL HIGH SCHOOL
WAYNESBURG, PA
TEACHER: STACIE PATTERSON

Suckston, Appalachia—
Coal bed streets kept alive by
100-watt stars, strung from insect tendrils,
Strung along a common vein,
Like the skeletal vestiges of some
Grandiose interstate cattle fence.

Specters shiver under newspaper linens
On these morgue slab nights—
Shadows of the proud forty-niners
Drown silently in a sallow vapor—
Sickly hues choking off the
Lovely helix of the Golden Arches

Hues seethed long ago, smoking from
Exhaust cloud sheen of a stainless steel hawk
Perched upon the Appalachian hillside
In the year of our lawd sixty-three—
Slapped down an asphalt slat,
Sprawled forth like a rotting rattlesnake
Piercing plains with chemical pungency . . .
Any ole fella will tell ya
Pastels of our Rockwellian landscapes
Began to streak toward the sunset that day . . .
Fervid was Suckston,

Bulging spider veins,
Outward engravings of an enclosed era,
Ripe for direct injection—
Dialysis into the city man's
Millennium frontiers!
Twenty breadths of IV wire,
Neon tubes jabbed in doublewides' flesh
Bleed out backwards brook of
Backwoods blood, carrion culture conveniently
Salvages—civilizes, serves in succulent sludge slather,
Suckston will ascend, all sermonize—
Our revolution will be pasteurized!

And once dried to a fine rust—
Settling o'er Suckston with certain malignancy,
Eyes glazing over to spackled sheen of
Broken windows in an abandoned mineshaft,
Mire of tin mausoleums, last living nomads
Stare staunch in pleasing fixations of rigor mortis,
Defrosting block chicken from the San Diego fires,
Bleeding into their living rooms from flickering glass,
Hazy apparitions of humanity
Seemingly return voyeur gazes
To the dutiful faces huddled 'round
Like frostbitten frontiersmen
Sprawled about a dying flame,
Before all succumb to private frigidness,
Reckoning of the second ice age . . .

HERE'S AN INCONVENIENT TRUTH: NO ONE CARES

ERIKA TURNER, 16

LIBERTY HIGH SCHOOL
HENDERSON, NV
TEACHER: JOSHUA WIKLER

Many people take to heart the fact that there are hundreds of political and activist groups on college campuses filled with passionate young adults striving every day to protest injustices and support "their cause," whatever it may be.

Yet, why does such fire only attribute itself to the over-18 age range? Why is it supposed that the well-being of American citizens should only be thought of once people can legally purchase both tobacco and alcohol?

Do we not care because high school students are unmerited toward any type of say in politics? We need a spirit of fire, a unilateral voice which most of us form, protesting the inadequacies of our education, the holes in our knowledge and the debts put upon us by the older generation.

A TWO-FOR-ONE WAR

In 2001, the century was welcomed in by a threat to U.S. security when the World Trade Center was attacked on September 11. The attackers were part of the international terrorist alliance Al Qaeda, based in Afghanistan and created by Osama Bin Laden in 1988. President George W. Bush launched a War on Terror in response to the attack.

On March 20, 2003, the Iraq War was launched in response to suspicions of tyrant Saddam Hussein harboring and creating weapons of mass destruction.

However, no weapons were found, and the war's purpose turned to bringing democracy to Iraq.

There are few people one could approach on the street who would know the difference between these two instances; there are very few who care.

It is a despairing fact that many of these people will soon be deciding the fate of this country upon graduation.

RETIREMENT? NOT AT THIS RATE

According to the *Las Vegas Review-Journal*, the first baby boomer (born in 1946) applied for her Social Security just four weeks ago. According to Social Security Commissioner Michael Astrue, since over 80 million children were born during the baby boomer era after World War II (1946-1964), about 10,000 people a day will become eligible for Social Security (i.e., insurance for temporary assistance and "supplemental security income" for persons over 65) over the next 20 years.

It is estimated that by 2041, the Social Security trust fund will run dry, which means that in 34 years, when most of us are only about 15 years from getting our social security (if everything else is peachy keen prior) . . . there will be none to collect.

It is a major concern and we don't even realize it.

AN INCONSOLABLE TRUTH: NO ONE CARES

We've all heard about it: Temperatures are rising all over the world. Sure, many scientists might say that global warming doesn't exist, but the fact that the amount of cateogry four and five hurricanes have nearly doubled in the last 30 years and over 300,000 people a year may begin to die due to its effects in the next 25 years should present the slightest bit of concern.

It is speculated that over a million species could become extinct and the Arctic Ocean could be ice-free in the summer of 2050.

Am I suggesting that we sport *An Inconvenient Truth* T-shirts made of hemp and attend the next Al Gore for President rally? No, of course not. What's being said is that we need to be more aware and more concerned.

REFORM AND REACT

At this point in our lives, our parents may be able to protect us from some things, but they can't stop Antarctica's ice from melting, can't stop our brothers and girlfriends and cousins from dying in war and they can't add millions of dollars to the national bank for our Social Security.

At least, not on their own.

We can no longer be content to stare blankly at our history teachers, quickly pass through the news channels and cruise the Internet for hours.

We cannot simply join a cause or two through the urging of MySpace or Facebook solicitors and then go on about our apathy after clicking out of the Web site.

Take a stand on more than just which band should be number one on MTV's TRL.

Read the newspaper, watch real, unbiased news, know what the USA PATRIOT Act and No Child Left Behind entail.

Be aware of the fact that we've been in two different wars in the last seven years and that we're approaching three, that Michael Moore isn't the sole source of truth and justice, that global warming may or may not exist, but that human trafficking and political corruption do.

Realize that New Orleans still has yet to recover from Katrina, even if the news isn't reporting on it and that more than just the little girl on the Chester Stiles video tape is a victim of abuse.

Remember that AIDS is still a major issue, as is teen pregnancy, racism, drug addiction and homelessness.

Oh, and by the way—where the hell is Osama?

We look through rose-colored glasses, thinking that we'll get involved when college rolls around, if even then. But life doesn't begin after graduation; certainly millions of people's have by then ended.

Being young is no excuse. In fact, it's the ultimate reason, because there's still time.

Remember, realize, read, and at the end of that?

Do.

THE TWO-MINUTE JOURNEY HOME WAS NOT, HOWEVER, WITHOUT ITS PROBLEMS

MARK WARREN, 17

TRINITY SCHOOL
NEW YORK, NY
TEACHER: CINDYLISA MUNIZ

By my estimation, I had uneventfully completed the block-and-a-half trek between my home and school 3,500 times. Every school day for the last ten years, I'd stepped over the same unusually wide crack in the sidewalk. I'd smelled the same rotisserie chickens cooking inside D'Agostino's. I'd heard the same old Puerto Rican guy talking to himself. Maybe I'd sprinted to beat a traffic light, or slowed down to watch a baseball game in the playground across the street, or stopped to make a snowball. But with 3,500 trips safely to and from Trinity School under my belt, I had no reason to believe that I would be beaten and robbed on the 3,501st trip.

"I've heard it's a great school," my mother's friend had once said, when I told her I went to Trinity. "But it's in a terrible neighborhood," she continued, unaware of my home's proximity to the school. Then, it was laughable; from my experience, my neighborhood was as safe as any I had ever been to. I'd been through my neighborhood by myself. I'd been through it with my parents. I'd been through it with white friends. I'd been through it with black friends. I'd been through it in the gray early morning. I'd been through it at three in the afternoon. I'd been through it at darkest midnight. I'd been through it in rain. I'd been through it in snow. I'd been through it carrying a four-by-six-foot poster of Roman Britain, with a not-to-scale, sugar-cube, Elmer's-glued-together Hadrian's Wall. And each trip, though different, was the same. Each trip I took care to step over the crack where the sidewalk rises an inch and becomes rougher. Each trip, as I passed the mural on the wall of D'Agostino's, I smelled the sharp aroma of chickens roasting. Each trip, as I passed the stoops of the brownstones, I listened to the elderly Puerto Rican mutter and mumble to himself. The journey had never been problematic.

On certain days off from school, too, I made the trip to school, if I'd left a book in my locker or I had an assignment saved on the computer at school. On this particular day off, the school's unused rooftop astro-turf field had sung its silent siren song and had attracted a sizeable group for a football game. There's no finale for a long weekend more fitting than some full-contact football.

I head straight home after the game. My turf-burned knees sting with each step, but they sting in a good way. I'll wash them off when I get home, and soon they'll be two dark-red badges of honor. As I cross Columbus Avenue this unseasonably warm Columbus Day afternoon, my mind is already in the movie theater where I plan to go after I wash off my knees and shower and change and do some homework and maybe have something to drink, and which is worse for you, the chemicals in diet soda or the sugar in regular?—a jarring blow to the right side of my face interrupts my train of thought. The pavement rushes up to meet me out of the left side of my vision. A dull thud resounds inside my head, but it could have been a mile away. I see stars, like in the cartoons. Only this is real.

I'm scared and confused. When I get up, do I fight my attacker? If he's smaller than I am, then sure, I can probably take him. But what if he's armed? And what's more, who could possibly have the chutzpah to attack me in broad daylight in the safest neighborhood I know—my neighborhood, where you know the smells and the cracks and the people?

Dizzy, I pull myself to my feet. But before I can even consider my options and get familiar with my already-familiar surroundings—surroundings I've known my whole life, surroundings I've always considered myself a part of—I'm knocked down again by a punch to the back of my head. Somebody kicks me while I'm down. Someone else goes through my pockets and takes my house keys, my phone, six dollars and thirteen cents, and a Canadian dime. I see a pair of black Adidas Campus ST's with white stripes. I see a cigarette butt. I see the half-inch wide crack where the sidewalk becomes less smooth. I see a tan Timberland boot. It kicks me in the side of the head and I black out.

When I come to a few seconds later, I stand up warily, and I see my aggressors run across 91st Street, dodging the sparse traffic. I look around myself frantically; surely somebody must have witnessed the attack. But I see nobody.

I continue my homeward odyssey. My legs feel like Jell-O. I feel like I've just had ten cups of coffee, and then had the mugs smashed on my head. I trip on the crack for the second time in 3,501 trips. I pass the old man. He wears a semitransparent mesh basketball jersey with nothing under it and a baseball cap emblazoned with the Puerto Rican flag. As I pass him, he points to my right ear. It's bleeding, and it stings. My knees sting, too, but they sting in a bad way now.

I try to act as if nothing has happened. I tell the doorman my injuries are from the football game. In the elevator, I close my eyes and compose myself, and fall apart, and compose myself again. How do you tell your mother, especially one as protective as yours, that despite all those safety talks, despite all those warnings—the letters home from the headmaster, the e-mails that have been circulated and forwarded to you—you've just been "accosted," to use the preferred euphemism. And it wasn't your fault. You weren't talking on your phone, you weren't wearing any flashy jewelry, you didn't have on any fancy clothes; you were just in the wrong place at the wrong time. But this infuriates you. It's your street. The smell is yours and the sidewalk is yours and even the old man is yours. Thirty-five hundred times you've walked this street and nothing's happened. But now, somehow, it's not yours anymore.

DEAD TREES
CHARLIE GREEN, 17
HARVARD WESTLAKE SCHOOL
NORTH HOLLYWOOD, CA
TEACHER: ERIC SCHRODE

The second-hand bookshop was down a narrow cobblestone street in Rome, near the flea market of Campo dei 'Fiori. Caught between dueling laundromats, the entrance was barely visible until passed. It was an afterthought, my turning back and reaching for the door. I had no idea that within this cramped façade I'd discover not only a book, but the start of a new chapter in my life.

I ducked inside mostly to escape the August heat wave pressing down on the city and on my mind. Painful memories had been rising in me the last few days, searing like the triple-digit temperature. The shop's AC, though tepid, was still a relief so I lingered, searching for something to read on the train. I'd rummaged through bins of novels and plays when I came across a thin volume: *The Waste Land* by T. S. Eliot. Only vaguely familiar with the poet, I wasn't sure what drew me to it: the smooth cover, the slender size, or maybe the price of the book, simply because it was marked in euros, which were romantically foreign to me. Purchasing the volume, I tucked it into my back pocket and headed to the Termini.

Once aboard the train, the pressing crowd and stagnant heat finally overwhelmed me, unleashing the dark thoughts I had wanted to forget. I sank back into my seat, closing my eyes, trying to escape discomfort within and without. But I was flooded with images of all I had seen in Italy: everything rang with a tragic history that resonated in my own life. In the Pieta I'd seen not Mary but my own mother, holding the limp and lifeless body of my older brother, dead for some ten years. On the far wall of the Sistine Chapel I saw Heaven and Hell and worried where God had destined my brother to spend eternity. At Pompeii I saw corpses, frozen in death, hands reaching toward Heaven but faces filled with the dread of Hell and I wondered, near tears, if perhaps my brother held the same expression buried so far away in a California cemetery.

Hanging my head as the heat surged through the compartment, I could hardly breathe. By now the train rushed down its track, the Italian countryside a blur outside the windows: dormant grape vines, fallow fields. I tried not to think about the dead, or other hounding memories that might still haunt me. Seeking escape, I pulled *The Waste Land* from my pocket and began to read.

I quickly became lost in the evocative words and beautiful imagery of Eliot's poem, immersed until I came across the passage: "For you know only a heap of broken images, where the sun beats, and the dead tree gives no shelter." It was that last line that really got to me . . . "The dead tree gives no shelter." Hit immediately on an emotional level, the intellectual power of the line did not register at first. Rereading the verse, Eliot's meaning became obvious: old and painful memories should not be dwelled upon for they offer us no comfort.

Not only was this an astute and brilliant line, but a philosophy that spoke to my current disposition with uncanny timing. Dwelling on my brother's death had sunk me into a melancholy state of mind throughout my stay in Italy. Instead of absorbing the beauty of the Pieta, the craft of the Sistine Chapel and the history of Pompeii, I could think only of my personal loss. I realized that I shouldn't let grief or painful memories blind me to the beauty of the Italian landscape, the freedom of summer, the possibilities of youth. If I were to spend my whole trip, indeed my whole life, living in the past, I would never enjoy the present or anticipate the future. I felt as if a window had finally opened and a serene breeze blew across my body.

As the train pulled into the station, I didn't put the volume back into my pocket when stepping out of the compartment. Instead, with

Eliot's masterpiece in hand and his words etched in my mind, I determined to look forward and embrace life with open arms.

Rather than close, as Eliot's *The Waste Land* did, with Shanith shanith shanith (the Peace which brings understanding), I feel it more appropriate to say instead that understanding can bring peace, as it has to me.

CURRENT
KEVIN HONG, 14
WALNUT HILL SCHOOL
NATICK, MA
TEACHER: DANIEL BOSCH

We walk past the gray stone of the roaring, broken-nosed lions and into Chinatown. Chinese pop music plays from speakers mounted on the lions' heads.

"How annoying," my mother says. "There is no substance to this— just crazy men screaming. Horrible. You are lucky I raised you well, Michael. I raised you to be a good boy."

We walk on the swollen cobblestones until we reach Elle's Beauty Salon.

"I have to do some shopping," my mother says. "I'll meet you inside. Be a good boy." She walks away, shoes clomping like a workhorse's.

Chimes sound unevenly above my head when I enter. Ring-a-chunk! Ring-a-ring-a-chunk! A rusty butterfly ricochets off chipped, bent metal tubes.

On the counter sits a picture frame displaying a "School of Barbering" certificate.

"Here for haircut?" the old man calls.

"Yeah."

"Five minute, please."

"Okay."

He is a chubby man, with jowls like a basset hound and thin lips. His comb-over is light gray, as if he glued gosling feathers to his head.

"We have not seen you for long time, only your father! Long hair in style, right?"

"Yeah."

The waiting area consists of five wooden stools and a coffee table.

Then come three leather barber seats on each side of the wall, with large mirrors in front of the seats. In the back of the salon, the washing station is covered in shadow, and a door leads to the pedicure room. Thin wire tubes hang seashell lamps from the ceiling, so low that I almost collide with one. The soft blue light doesn't match the rest of the place—cheap tiles, posters of haircuts to hide the water stains on the walls. Stay cool! Stay hot! and Give your hair volume!

I sit on a wooden stool and flip through the Chinese magazines until I find English. *Walt Disney's American Classics: Davy Crockett*. I skim through the brown baby bears, the battle of the Alamo. Then *Automobile*, *Golf Digest*, and cartoons of *Monkey King: Journey to the West*.

See monkey. See monkey jump. See monkey study and become strong. See monkey steal ancient weapon. See monkey piss on Buddha's hand. See monkey get smashed by big mountain.

"Come!" says the old man, leaning casually on the washstand, grinning wide. Bags under his eyes, as if he needs to hold all his extra happiness somewhere.

The reclining chair is comfy. I lean back against the porcelain sink. The showerhead looks like an electrocution device. I used to have dreams about being tortured. I'd have wires attached to my neck, and a man would send electric charges through me. He'd say, "Do you surrender?"

I'd shake my middle finger at him. "Screw you."

Gradually, I'd give in.

"Switching school?" the old man says.

His breath smells of anchovies, his sweater faintly of cats.

"Yeah, I'm going to Boston," I say.

"Your father told me," he says, and scratches hard on my scalp. I wince; he smiles. His crooked, leathery hands lather the shampoo. He digs in with his claws.

"Lift," he says.

I strain upward for a minute while he runs foam through my hair.

The shampoo seeps into my eyes. I sniffle from the burn. My father would say it builds character. Anything that doesn't kill you makes you stronger. He told me of a man who believed this, who used to eat rats. Raw.

"Down."

I ease back.

"Your friends know?"

"Huh?"

"Have you told your friends you go away? You have big party?"

"Uh. No," I say.

And that's the truth. I've never liked parties. I can't dance. Everyone shimmies and does the Harlem shake or whatever it is, and I can't even sway to the beat. I can't eat and socialize at the same time; I choke or spit food. Worst of all is the attention, especially on birthdays. Everyone grinning, singing, looking at me. Knowing that they're there because of me, and if they're not happy it's my fault, and if they are happy I still never have a good time because people are pushing me to do things—blow the candles out, serve the cake, smile, smile, say thank you, smile.

The old man lathers, scratches, rinses, scratches, and rinses again. He wraps a towel around my head like a turban and pats my back.

"Wait over there."

I sit back down on a stool and look at a male model on the cover of a Chinese magazine. Hair dyed rusty orange, layered into ruffles. He's posing with hands on hips, one foot in front of the other, black magic in his eyes. I wonder if he's as suave in real life as he appears on the cover. Behind all that makeup and crazy hair, maybe he goes home to an old mother and tries to coax oatmeal into her. Maybe his girl left him. Or maybe she's dead. Maybe the old hag will die too. Then he'll be all alone.

I know what my father would say. That's life. Life, death, and forgetting about it.

"Come!" the old man says.

I sit down on a swivel chair and a tall lady takes over. Her plastic nametag says: Anna Tam—Expert Stylist. She looks like a tired Furby: the rims of her eyes are loaded with mascara. Her hair is long, puffy and dyed pink. Front teeth jut from her lips. She flings a covering over me, cinches it at my neck.

"It's tight," I say.

"No worry, no worry! That's the way it's supposed to be."

Ring-a-chunk, ring-a-ring-a-chunk.

My mother stands inside the entrance, clutching grocery bags. She stomps her feet on the welcome mat, even though it's not wet outside, and she shakes her head. Her hair is short; each morning, she sprays it stiff as my father's starched collars.

"Has he been a good boy?" she asks.

"Oh, yes!" the stylist replies. "What cut does he want?"

"A trim, please," I say.

"He wants it very short," my mother says, leaning on the counter.

"Not too short," I say.

"No, of course not," the stylist says, and tilts her head, smiling sadly at my mother, who mimics the gesture. I shake my head and take off my glasses. My face smears in the mirror like pastel.

Raucous laughter outside; it seems so far away. A group of teenagers slurp smoothies and clutch the dragon columns. I imagine my drunk, rosy-cheeked friends laughing and vomiting out the windows, the twisted faces of passers-by.

I look at the fat, laughing Buddha embedded in the soil of a potted-plant. Above his head he balances on his pinkies a large, gold piece. Like an anvil, it threatens to drop. The Buddha smiles.

The stylist takes a squirt bottle and shoots at my head. Mist descends, cools my cheeks. I close my eyes.

I want to go home and sleep. The tulips are supposed to be in full bloom, only they never grow right in my yard. They bud quickly and blossom for a day before they are weighed down by their heavy petals, flopping to one side like an opossum playing dead. It's easy for them to give up. They'll always rise again.

The tulips in our neighbor's yard are beautiful, though. My window overlooks their garden. I want to gaze at them and then sleep.

Every day I wonder where my friends went when they died. I asked my dad and he said everyone disintegrates into atoms and fertilizes the grass.

"Really?" I asked. "What about heaven?"

He told me there is no heaven. No God—just conscience.

"How do you know conscience isn't God talking to you?"

He told me I was stupid. God wouldn't tell the terrorists to kill.

I wasn't with my friends when they died. They wanted me to come, but I refused. I don't drink. I have my mother's "good boy" mentality. Sometimes I wish I had been with them.

The car they were in swerved off a small bridge and they all drowned. Knowing them, they probably died laughing. CNN said two of them had perfect scores on the ACT. FOX News criticized the driving age.

The river is calm and clear; it reflects the pale-blue sky, but you can almost see to the bottom. It is no more than ten feet deep. The stones are round, smooth, perfect for skipping. There are no more signs of death. Sometimes you can see the minnows darting back and forth like tiny pinballs. And the moss growing on the rocks; the green is taking on a gray hue from the roadside pollution.

The stylist pats my head. "You'll look handsome after this. Like a little Buddha."

"Please, not too short," I say.

The stylist laughs. "You'll look good. I promise."

"My hips don't lie," the radio sings in a velvet voice.

The stylist turns my head side to side, peering closely. All imperfections are exposed; the heart-shaped birthmark in my ear, the faint (and prominent) pimples, scars from tackle football.

"You have many red bumps," the stylist says, poking my face. "I see now why you had long hair—to hide the ones on your forehead!"

"Thanks," I say. I just want to sink into this chair and sleep.

My father says it's all about the outer image. People hire you for your three-piece suit, for your gold-plated business card. He says I should take posture classes.

"Excited for school?"

"Yes," I say.

"Your father told me last time he came," she says. I try to see what she's done with my hair, but all I can see is a blazing pink ghost hovering over me. "In three months, you will be away from family! It's like college, but so much earlier!"

I look at my mother. She is standing straight, arms crossed over chest.

"You should be proud of him," the stylist says. "So mature!"

My mother smiles. "He is a good boy," she says, as always.

My parents didn't say much when we found my friends had died. It was six o'clock; we were watching the news, eating fried rice and take-out Japanese. There were shootings at a college—some kid went on a rampage. I hope this doesn't make me sound like a jerk, but I didn't feel for the victims. Or the killer, for that matter. I didn't feel pity, or fear—nothing. I knew I should; I really wanted to. But I just didn't. Even when they found the killer's twisted stories about his teachers—about rape and chainsaws, I didn't feel anything.

"Horrible. Just horrible," my mother said.

My father said that I should go to a psychiatrist to make sure I wouldn't do something like that. It was clear that God couldn't stop these things. The kid was Catholic.

Then the river flashed on screen. Murky, and that alone, that soiled, familiar image, shocked me. My jaw wouldn't chew.

Toby's car was in the river; the trunk and one wheel showing above the surface. Dragonflies buzzed rainbows, tails rippling the water, wings lighting on and off. Pictures of my friends appeared. Their class photos. They were smiling, wearing white shirts and skinny neckties.

"Four teenagers, Tony Gao, Martin Zhou, Benjamin Silverstein and Richard Liu from Morrison High in the West Loop of Chicago drowned today. Police found alcohol in the trunk. We are—"

My mother turned off the TV and looked at me. I felt her eyes breaking me down. Wasabi rushed up my nose; I wheezed.

"Good boy, good boy, don't cry," my mother said, but I did.

I cried for a long time. Silently, although it was hard to keep from screaming. My mother said she was sorry, and made me tea, saying "Good boy, good boy," all the while. I tried to drink it, but I couldn't keep from trembling; the tea burbled with every sharp breath and choked me.

My father sat with me for a long time, his arm around my shoulders. When I stopped crying, I asked him, coughing in between words, "Why did God let this happen?"

He said that there is no God. Just life and death and forgetting about it.

■

Buzz. The razor hovers close to my ear lobe. It tickles, and I struggle not to move.

"What a sweetie," the stylist says.

"Yes," my mother agrees. "Good boy. Good boy."

"Boston school!" the stylist says. "I can't imagine! It is hard to be away from parents. You must tell yourself to study and do work. Kids these days . . . "

The stylist drones on in her machine-gun Chinese and I close my eyes.

"It wears me out," Thom Yorke wails on the radio. "Just turn and run . . ."

The stylist finally sends me back to the hair-washing station, where the old, scruffy man takes over again. He smacks his lips on his mint like he doesn't have teeth to chew. He takes the shower head and places it on my hairline. Warm water gushes over my face. I shiver.

"Leaving soon," he says.

"Yes."

"Many memories you keep."

"Yes." I feel like crying. Memories. Goddamn memories.

"You know," he says, "I will miss you." He swallows his mint; his lips are thin and faint pink. "Not because you are customer. I know you for many years now. You remind me of my friend."

"Oh."

He combs loose hairs from my head. "Yes, I had friend like you, many years ago. He live close to here. American man. He was quiet. Very quiet, always out of circle, observing. Lift."

I lift my head.

"We go to bars and listen to jazz. I liked oldies, Count Basie and such. He like Marsalis and Davis. Sometimes they played Beatles record.

"We had drinks and sit in corner, me staring into my beer, him looking at couples laughing, drinking, kissing. He don't talk, just took quick sip and roll the taste in his mouth, slowly. Very slow. His eyes, his eyes . . . well, I don't know. Down."

I lower my head. He moves the spout along my brow. The heat courses down to my toes. He squirts more shampoo into his hands, lathers it slowly, taking care that nothing escapes from his palms.

"His eyes," I say.

"Right. His eyes. Not maturity, I think. Maybe sadness; he always thinking, and he never tell me what about. Before he die of sickness, he tell me he is thinking about his wife. Who die years ago. He is convince that he is reason she died. He never put things behind him. Lift."

He rubs shampoo on the back of my head, gently massaging my nape. His touch isn't so rough. It is strong, but slow and smooth, like he's letting me know, ever so gently, that he is here, now, in the moment, like jumping naked into the river. Diving in and succumbing to the cold, letting the current take you under the bridge, past the school, real slow, everything deep in the water.

"When he look out at those couples, he always miss his wife. Want her beside him. Want her to lay her head on his shoulder, you know. Tap her fingers on her scotch to beat of jazz.

"When his wife alive, they dance to tunes. They always dance to 'Wild Man.' I mean, him and his wife, they smooth as cats. They like to jitterbug—just go crazy." He laughs. "Down."

A fast rinse—then conditioner.

"After she die, he want to dance. He really do. He want to shake and jump and—what do you call it these days?"

"Grind?"

"Yeah. Guh-line. He want to be free in movements, in moment, you know? But he couldn't. He try to dance, but he can't. Could not move on. Always cry when 'Wild Man' play."

He lets out a big sigh, and I take in the mint-anchovy breath.

"Before he die, he ask me if I think he will go to heaven. And I told him yes, if he believe. And he said no. He say he won't go to heaven, say he is bad man."

"And he's dead now?"

"Yes. Now he is dead."

The old man sighs. "I not talking about forgetting. Impossible to forget the ones you love. But I talk about letting go. Two different things. I still remember 'Wild Man' and jitterbug and, you know, the beer froth pop on my nose. But life go on, you know? We have job to do and future to make, and pork and leek dumplings in evening." He chuckles. "If you relive same moment again and again, you become dust. Got to live, you know? Live in current time. And the close ones who left—they are forever watching."

The last rinse is long. The old man is smiling ever so faintly; the tip of his snaggletooth pokes from his mouth. Eyes closed, he takes his time running his fingers through my hair; water droplets massage my eyes, tickle my earlobes, and caress my cheeks, softly as a baby's touch. A tingling sensation lingers like a cat's warm nuzzle.

■

The sun is setting; pink claws the sky as we step out of Elle's Beauty Salon. We pass the stone-gray locks of the rearing lions. During the drive home, Shostakovich blasts on the radio. A Buddha bobbles his head on the dashboard.

"Pay attention to the dynamics," my mother says. "The change of mood."

From the window of my bedroom, I gaze at the yellow tulips next door. Bright, like fairy lanterns, they dance with the evening breeze. My tulips will survive next year—no doubt about it. I sleep, and I dream of drifting past friends, past school, flowing with the current— everything here and now and deep in the water.

ON AMERICAN IDENTITY

DINA ABDULHADI, 16

CHATTAHOOCHEE HIGH SCHOOL
ALPHARETTA, GA
TEACHER: SHELLY SCHER

America can be defined with many words: not just the terminology of freedom and democracy, not just relative affluence. America is defined by its contrasts, its lack of a defining, objective perception of its identity, the multiple opposing forces working against each other at any given time, coexisting but strained in their efforts.

America is what we perceive as virgin soil, without past civilization ingrained in the land (for any history was carried away long ago with the Trail of Tears, with the flooding of Indian graves), based on an ethereal transplantation of a society from far across the dark ocean, translucent, ephemeral and intangible, ungraspable and not fit to internalize and make a part of one's identity quite as well as wished.

America is the gritty existentialism found in the dirt-coffee cups of dingy, working-class diners in rainy, postwar cities. America is the mundane and the romanticized: the blue-collar workers, the bright city lights, the streets like Broadway Musicals. America is a moment's chance at infinity, the fulfillment of one's potential and one's potential fulfillment. But it's still the small towns that seem connected to the rest of the world only by cold wired connections and a single dirt road, the cynical youth found in suburbia, angry at their parents and all of the cardboard-box houses, and able to afford the luxury of that jaded disdain. It's as much Lincoln Park as Cabrini Green, but not as much rich as poor, statistically speaking.

America is the Puritan land facing the cold, vast ocean, self-isolating and somber, the human silhouette against the ocean's storming sky. America is the first shot at Lexington and Concord, the rebel's cry, the sniper's shot in the back, the start of something new. America is its own Manifest Destiny spread from sea to shining sea, killing and slashing through the flesh and the dirt of what was there and what had been there along the way. America is the War Between the States, the internal strife arising from all of these multiplicities and insecurities based on an undecided foundation. America is the world wars, still tied to the Old World and the rest of humanity as much as it would like to deny it sometimes. It's as much the Great Depression as recession and inflation and the failing of the American Dream. It is fear of apocalyptic Cold War nuclear annihilation, as much duck and cover as hope placed in the futility of resistance. It speaks as much of power as of intervention, as much of corruption as of protection of a way of life and a way of thinking that is not necessarily essentially American, but an aspect of it nonetheless.

America is a road trip on long, straight and calculated interstates through plains of grass for bison turned wheat for humans turned soy for biofuel for machines. America is as much Cape Cod as Camden, as much the KKK as lazy southern afternoons that tend to transcend into fantasy as languid as a southern drawl. It's as much of a whirlwind of change as it is steady and consistent in its idea of what America is.

America is what we want it to be.

TO WAIT IN ROME
AVITAL CHIZHIK, 16
BRURIAH HIGH SCHOOL FOR GIRLS
ELIZABETH, NJ
TEACHER: MARGUEYA NOVICK

i was slowly becoming a banana, and the italians weren't helping. days slid by like gondolas, so slow and aggravating, my young strong body bursting to see the streets of america. and all we ate were bananas, only five-hundred tiny liras for each one, when you buy them on via di maria magdalena. no cheese or meat. just some black bread and bananas and water.

we found out, after a week in rome, that aunt asya and my little cousins and babulya and ded were denied a visa. denied, just like that. a visa is denied, a name, a life.

when mama found out, she cried until her tears mingled with the milk of her breast and little suckling tanya began to cry from the saltiness of her breakfast.

the shubkins who shared our room came out and sat quietly like good leningrad-ers do. and i left and sat and waited on the doorstep of our run-down hotel that smelled like too many people, pulling my short dress over my white knees and resting my chin on my hand.

i heard quick footsteps down the staircase inside and saw mama, in her old worn heels and flung-on jacket, clutching her purse and rushing out. she did not see me. i could hear tanya's cries upstairs and mrs. shubkin's whispers.

there were two-and-a-half jews in my class in kharkov.

one was my red-haired friend rima and one was that annoying boris with his dimples and brushed-over hair, and the half was vova, who always knew the right answer and who sent me love notes through his little sister.

i pretended that i didn't read the scribbled papers, but when no one was looking, i'd sit and read them over and over, giggling like one of those pixies in the fairy tales.

mama spent the next three days in every church in rome. papa tried to forget her and spent his time at every free attraction in the city. i gathered tanya and wandered around the streets with her in my arms, or sometimes put her down and let her walk with her little top-top steps. and at every passing church, i'd wonder if my mother was inside, praying to some foreign god.

back home in kharkov, there were two old ladies, one-eyed dounia ivanovna and cabbage-skinned raya isaakovna. they sat on our building's front porch, pretending to be chewing sunflower seeds—deaf to all around. yet they somehow knew everyone's headaches and romances and poor grades.

i was secretly terrified of them; every time i left for school and came back, they'd be sitting there. dounia would send her evil eye after me, so when i came home mama would make me change out of my contaminated clothing. and that cabbage, raya, would sit there shouting blessings—"may you live until you die!"—casting curses like a naked winter tree casts forth its branches.

all the children from the courtyard would make bets on how long they sat there, the eye and the cabbage, the ukrainian and the jew. we'd plan to sneak out of our beds at midnight to try to catch them boiling rats, but never ventured far down the creaking hallways, the peeling staircase.

the night before we left the soyuz, we slept on the floor and left right before dawn. our few belongings were packed already, and mama and papa led us out on tiptoes, like in hide and seek.

as we left the building, i heard sunflower seeds cracking and a crow-ing whisper, may you live until you die, may you die until you live.

at the jewish center they told us that we were jews. but i knew that, because the kids in my class never forgot to remind me of that.

but we weren't just zhids, we were jews, which meant that we had holidays and music, a country and a history.

they told us that almost forty years ago, the germans killed many jews. how many? they said six million but that is too much. if it was some big number like that, we would have known.

in kharkov, the door to our building's courtyard was always open. it was a green haven, between the light-colored walls and the old foun-tain in the middle. children planted whispering orchids every spring, and at night we'd sit on the rusty balcony and watch the young cou-ples laugh and dance.

to be surrounded by candles,
and browns and pictures of people in gentle robes,
a pure mother holding open her arms,
embracing the world with a sad smile.
mama would kneel in the front pew of a church, crying and praying,
even though we were supposed to be jews,
we had our own place to pray, we were told.
the synagogue.
i'd sit in the back and watch her cry.
she never knew that I followed her around to the cathedrals.
it must have been that strange, unpleasantly sweet smell
which drew her to the doors of the church,
or the soft chanting of the monks,
or maybe just the virgin in all her kindness
who promised to understand mama's sorrow

and to save aunt asya and the little cousins and babulya and ded.

but the virgin must have been too busy to help mama and us.
or, i thought, if it wasn't our place to pray to the madonna.
or maybe, she was just a pretty picture.
mama must have thought this, too, because soon i saw her putting
on a kerchief and running to the old synagogues. not the new one at the
jewish center, but the ancient ones
with high ceilings and stone walls.
and when she came back from there, she'd also be red and teary.
just like in the churches.

so strange it was
to be taught one minute that there is no god
that it is the party and only the party
to be worshipped,
and then we're told that we have a god, our own.
i wondered what people did when they were sad back in the soyuz.
to whom did they pray?

i asked papa this once, during a quiet lunch with the shubkins,
when mama was not home. he said that people did not pray, they drank.
he told me that a nation so steeped in drink is a nation steeped in sorrow. i asked him if he believed in god, and he said no.

i once had a stamp collection. beautiful colors, renaissance paintings
and french palaces that played vivaldi in their ballrooms and had ladies
in hoop gowns and powdered wigs. i started collecting when i was
eight, but now, after two years of rummaging through the mail for
new additions to my album, mama and papa forbid me from taking it
along. who knows what trouble we can get into, carrying postage
money across the soviet border? mama consoled me and told me that

i can start all over again in america, where no doubt they have prettier stamps. but i don't plan on it. my stamps i had in russia, and that is where i left them.

on friday night mr. shubkin would take out his guitar and play for us. he emptied his suitcase of clothing and books, just so he'd have room for his guitar, his wife told us. shabbes shabbes shabbes shabbes koydesh, he sang, and we'd all join in: zol zayn zol zayn zol zayn shabbes. such a strange song, that even mr. shubkin didn't understand it. "my father sang it," he told us. and so we'd sit there and sing in a cramped room in rome, singing a song which no one understood.

they pretended to teach us english at the center. good morning. dozens of us sat in the hall and copied the teacher's loud intrusive words. nice to meet you. anyone under the age of nine went to the playgroup for an hour. i am from russia, i don't speak english. i'd sit and pass notes with the other girls i met there—mashsa, lena, vera. it is sunny outside. they told us to say in russian, "daniel, take the ball," and it will mean thank you in english. danka beri mach.

at the age of ten, i became a thief.
i knew it was wrong, but how could we sell our books? only tolstoy and pushkin would go with us, but what about my astrid lindgren books? and my mary poppins, and robinson crusoe, and my colorful fairy tales? every day, i'd peek in the boxes that mama and papa packed up to sell, and take out another book. i watched them sort and sigh, laugh and whisper over old books and notes that were slipped in between the pages. "remember," mama said to papa, taking dried flowers out of a dostoevsky, "how we picked these in kiev?" and then papa would open up a lermentov, and point to the inscription. "my mother, may she rest in peace, gave this to me on my fourteenth birthday," he'd say, and then he'd close it, kiss it, and slowly put it in the box. we left

everything behind, but our books—that was the most heartbreaking.

the airplane which would take us to new york smelled like stale air fresheners, but we didn't care. papa told us that in america, it would be clean and good-smelling everywhere you went. even in the bathrooms? i asked.

tanya and i liked the rumble of the plane when it began to take off. we waved our hands to the rhythm, laughing quietly, while papa smiled and reread his book. but mama was quiet, her kerchief shaking and her eyes white, looking past three seats, at the closest window. and in that glass, i saw the europe that we were leaving, i saw two-and-a-half jews, and a cabbage and an eye, and an empty whispering doorway and a confused guitar, and myriads of postage stamps and bananas.

i looked at mama, and i saw her lips move, in a silent prayer.

DARE
GRACE MCNAMEE, 14

GEORGETOWN DAY SCHOOL
WASHINGTON, D.C.
TEACHER: JOHN BURGHARDT

Despite the persistent rumors to the contrary, my grandpa didn't die driving his Chevy across the pond. For one thing, my grandpa wouldn't drive that rusty red pickup across the pond; he cares too much about it. For another thing, he's not dead.

But believe what you want to believe.

We did drive across the pond, of course. But we did that often, it's not hard. Course Grandpa would never take the pickup—it's not built for it, and Grandpa loved that thing.

It was very cold that night, and my dad's Mazda only has heat during the summer and AC during the winter. Being out on the pond didn't matter.

Grandpa would say I'm ruining a perfectly good story right about now. He'd interrupt me and tell me to tell it right or not tell it at all. And so I wouldn't tell it, not past the part I'd already said. Grandpa would take over, grossly exaggerating every particular of the story.

He'd say the pond was a lake. He'd say that the car became waterlogged and started to sink. He'd play hero. That's why we drove across the pond, he hoped to be a hero.

That particular night was in mid-December, and Grandpa had turned the AC on full blast. We sat on the edge of the road in the Mazda, freezing and staring out at the water. Grandpa always said it was daring us. He would tell me that only a chicken wouldn't take the dare. He always pointed out that you could see the other side. But you can't really, not when you're on the water. When you're on the road you can, but the road's on a hill, from the road you could probably see New

York City, all the way from the salt marshes of Washington state.

He glanced over at me after we'd sat there for what he considered long enough—12 minutes, as always.

"Should we do it?" he asked me, poking buttons on the broken radio and adjusting his old brown coat. I'd bought him a new coat once, with my mom's help, but he still wore the brown tattered one. I've never seen him in the coat I bought him, I think he sold it or something. It was like the truck: He didn't care how old and broken it was, he would wear it until it fell off of him.

"No," I replied, as always, glancing out over the water. It was so wonderful to Grandpa and so horrifying to me.

"He's calling to us," he informed me sternly, revving the engine for dramatic effect. The AC sputtered and got colder, if that was possible.

"My cell phone's turned off. I didn't get his call."

"It's rude not to accept the invitation of an old friend."

Grandpa's old friend was a mile across. It was 11 at night and the water was black as midnight. Even if Grandpa's chance came that night, he wouldn't be able to see well enough to play hero.

But the car was already thundering down the hill. That was the one good part of the whole crossing-the-pond-in-Dad's-half-dead-Mazda. We were shooting straight downhill in an out-of-control car, the water was rushing at us, reaching for a hug, the windows were wide open and Grandpa was screaming like it was all a great ride. To him, all life's a ride, has been since my grandmother died. That was the first time Grandpa drove across the pond, the day of my grandmother's funeral. He wouldn't go to the funeral, and he wouldn't let me. So we drove across the pond instead.

About the time we hit the water, Grandpa pulled the car out of neutral.

If I ever got this far in telling the story, he'd tell me that wasn't right. He'd claim he JERKED the car into gear, saving both our skins. He'd also make me leave out the part where he insisted that we go across—he'd say it was one of my harebrained schemes, especially if my mother was listening.

What matters is, when the car first hit the water, Grandpa put it in four-wheel drive, slamming his foot on the gas, laughing his head off as the tires spun wildly. For a few short moments it always seemed like we were about to sink, every time it felt that way, whether you expected it or not. But the engine roared and the tires spun and we were driving wildly across Grandpa's old friend.

The wind and salt and water and noise were everywhere, impossible not to hear and feel and taste. The noise would have been deafening if it wasn't soothing, the reminder that we were driving across the pond.

And that's when Grandpa would start to sob.

The first time I wasn't surprised, not on the day of Grandma's funeral. The first time it was natural for him to cry like a baby. The second time it was a surprise. By the third time I'd learned not to comfort him. By the fourth I'd learned to move him into the passenger seat and drive the spluttering car to the other side. I only sank the car at the very end, when everything was too waterlogged to move, when Grandpa was just sitting still, staring at the depths of his old friend as if they were hiding heaven. And that's when I'd dive in and push the car the last few feet.

It's always cold. No matter what the season, that water is always cold.

That last time Grandpa opened the door, stepping out onto the dry land on the edge of the pond in silence. He stood staring out at the water, not seeing me, sitting on the trunk of the car, shivering. When he turned he looked haunted.

The old Grandpa would tell me that that wasn't right. He'd claim he was tired after towing the car out of the water single-handedly. He'd claim I couldn't see right because I was dizzy or sick. But that Grandpa wasn't there that night. That Grandpa wouldn't have walked home drenched. That Grandpa wouldn't have gotten in his pickup and driven off. That Grandpa wouldn't have left me on the bank of the pond, waiting for a tow truck.

This Grandpa didn't come back from his road trip for weeks. By then, everyone was swearing they saw him drown when he tried to drive across the pond. Grandpa never tried to correct that story.

"That pond's daring me, you know," he told me once when we were driving past in his pickup. "It's daring me to go insane."

I DON'T WANT TO SLAM

HAYDIL HENRIQUEZ, 16

DREAM YARD PREPARATORY
BRONX, NY
TEACHER: ARACELIS GIRMAY

I don't want to slam
The innocence imprinted in my face tells tales of lack of creativity
My creativity is blindfolded by the college application rejection that
    I must receive
Cascaded
Deteriorated
From acid rain continuously jumping into the rigid vivid declaration
    of failure
To tell you the truth
Yo, I, Je
I'm afraid of failure
P.R.I.D.E. is my major priority
I don't want to commit to crashing voices screaming to be liberated
    by poetry's lullaby
So later I let myself down by misleading broken corpses
Into the public inferno of a mind-bottled convention
Imprisoned in their train wreck lives

I started a precedent a little while back
That now runs every thought in every second of my life
I don't want to quit
And I'm not
Because poetry is this indescribable gift that I know I must share

My lines gleam, glare, and glide
Show a glee a glimpse of glisten
Not a glob or a glop but gild
They turn on and on and on and their limit is the number above
    infinity
And I must tell my grandkids' grandkids
About how normal things evolve differently in my mind
Music notes swing dance as horses on my sheets
They galloped into perfection and its imperfections were ignored
Wings didn't mean freedom but escapes of 32-year-old dictatorships
    on a forgotten island
And home wasn't a touchable place with four walls
But the occult broken road to the paradise of heaven

I am a daydreamer that has too much on her mind
And plans even simple conversations
That I often derive
But poetry destroys all those mind-haunting plans for the while I am
    at room 425
And that's a good thing
Cause I'm tired of a planned life
Of grammar corrected conjunctions in simple sentences
While verbs and subjects differ
But I'm still not ready to slam
Because my confidence has reached its lowest point
Which is kind of a point above -12 in my thermometer of 3
I lost my mojo
I lost my individuality
I missed the evoking call of randomness on my fingertips
The wind of knowledge undulating impatiently under my flesh
I can't think straight and words never splice with their proper punc-
    tuation or make sense

I stare at the word "for" for four hours and I still don't get what it
    means
My knowledge has reached a rudimentary level now
And I cannot even obtain it back
But today I learned poets never settle for less
And they don't give up in a storm full of regrets
Poets are the John Lockes of writing
The Ghandis of humanity
Poets are superior to nightmares
Poets are the brain cerebral cortex that holds complete sentences
    together
Of telling the world its corrupted lies continuously stab the brains of
    children
That live every day miserably
Because sanctions in Burma prevent them from eating 200 calories a
    day
And the bomb dust inhalant kills nerve cells on Tuesday
And I accept the spreading of the word
The poet's way

THE SIZE OF A SMALL COFFIN

BECKY MCCARTHY, 18

GREENS FARMS ACADEMY
GREENS FARMS, CT
TEACHER: ELIZABETH CLEARY

"Like, for example, finding out who you're going to marry," Rita says, kicking off her heels so they skid across the dirty linoleum. There are holes in the toes of her stockings. "You're supposed to kill a black chicken—I think it's a chicken. Some sort of poultry anyway. Kill it and throw it over your shoulder at midnight at a three-way crossroad where a murderer is buried. Then you say something to the devil and put the dirt from your footprints in a bottle. Sleep with the bottle under your pillow, and you'll dream the name of your intended."

"Just say anything to the devil?" I say, "or does it have to be something specific?" She shrugs, handing me coffee in a Three Stooges novelty mug. It's day-old instant coffee, reheated in the microwave and an iridescent film covers the top like an oil slick.

"I think there was something specific," she says, "but the devil doesn't really seem like the kind of guy who'd get hung up on formalities." She drags her purse toward her by the strap and pulls out a tiny, tapestry-covered makeup bag. Rita has a friend who works the cosmetic counter at the pharmacy and gives her the standard gift bags and promotional paraphernalia without making her buy anything. As a result, most of her makeup is oddly colored. She applies lipstick without a mirror, the way my mom used to. I read Tangerine Dream across the bottom of the tube.

"My grandma had a whole book of those," she says. "Folk spells and superstitions. That one's not particularly helpful, though. I mean, what—I'm just supposed to stumble upon a three-way crossroad where a murdered is buried? You know any of those?"

I shake my head. "Sorry," I say. The tapestry on her makeup bag is a miniature of those famous ones I learned about in elementary school. The Hunt of the Unicorn. Rita pretends to fix her hair so she can sneak another glance at the clock.

"Tell me another one," I say, to distract her. She looks down at her coffee and pretends not to notice what I'm doing.

"I shouldn't drink this," she says, tapping the mug. "I don't want coffee breath," I get up and pour both of ours down the drain.

"Tell me another one," I say.

I am supposedly here to use Rita's computer to do my taxes, but I am really here to say, "You should wear your hair like that more often" and, "Where'd you get that shirt?" I am here to calm pregame jitters, to say, "Maybe wait till you get to the restaurant to start on the wine." I am here to pretend to be confused by my tax reports, to wait for her to come home and to grin suggestively at work tomorrow if she doesn't. I am here to commiserate if it goes badly. Am here in case it goes worse than badly—in case it goes well. In case he's not a con-victed felon or obese or living with his mother, and still doesn't kiss her goodnight. I am here to laugh when she is not funny and direct all expression of pity toward him instead of her.

"If you want to win at cards," she's saying, "stick a crooked pin in your coat. If you need money, make a purse from weasel's skin. If you're being chased by an evil spirit of a ghost and you hear footsteps behind you, try and cross some sort of stream of running water and they won't be able to follow you.

"Have you actually tried any of these?" I ask. She shakes her head, her earrings catching the light and spraying rainbows all over the cabinets.

"Nah," she says, "I still have the book somewhere, though." She is running her nails under the edge of the table, pulling up the plastic lining glued over the corkboard. It is quarter to nine and he is a half hour late and all I want to do is make up an excuse to leave in order to save her the embarrassment of having to admit to me that he is not coming. But Rita is imagining a future in which this guy turns out to be The Guy, in which he smiles up at her over the cake and says Remember our first date? How you thought I'd stood you up?

■

Last year for her birthday I got together some people from work and took her out to that club in town, the one with all the aspiring Chippendales. It was supposed to be funny, but three drinks into the night she started to cry. Sobbing, uncontrollably, on her 28th birthday, in the middle of a club, surrounded by coworkers she didn't like and gay men in assless chaps.

■

Eight years ago, when Rita was my age, she got pregnant by some guy she was dating who sold vacuum cleaners.

"I was going to get rid of it," she told me, "but it was so expensive and I kept putting it off and then, you know, time's up and it's too late." She had shrugged. "I guess I kind of wanted it." We were sitting in a booth at the T.G.I. Friday's down the street. The streetlight was shining through the window and the falling rain threw its shadow over our table and across our hands like spectral smallpox.

"What happened?"

"It died," she said. "Eight months in. It just died. It was weird; I didn't think that happened anymore. Like stillborns were strictly an 18th-century thing." She laughed. "I felt like such an asshole. Because, you know, I bought all these baby clothes. Dresses and frilly overalls and shoes; I even bought a fucking American Girl doll. Because I always wanted one when I was a kid. And they cut her out of me and asked me if I wanted to hold her. Sometimes they tell you not to, you know, if the kid's already dead, bit I did. And they wrapped her up in a blanket and put this little bow in the tiny tuft of hair she had, and as soon as I saw her I realized how stupid everything I'd done had been. You know? I mean, what did I do for my daughter? I ordered her an American Girl doll. A doll. I should've been getting sonograms once a day, I should've called up a witch doctor. Something." The waitress brought our food to the table. I wasn't hungry, but Rita ate like she was starving.

"Don't feel sorry for me," she said, around a mouthful of hamburger.

■

"Tell me another one," I say. She has pulled up the edges of the table lining entirely and there is black cork under her fingernails.

"There is one moment," she says, "in every day when whatever you wish will be granted, but no one knows what that moment is. It's only by chance that you can come upon it."

"Those aren't such bad odds," I say. "I mean it's not like it's once a year."

"Yeah," she says. "I just keep missing it."

■

The doll came in the mail the day after the funeral, she told me. She left it out in the rain for a week until they took it away with the garbage.

That is not the truth, though. Not the whole truth, because last year when I was helping her look for Christmas lights I found a warped American Girl box stuffed all the way in the back of her bedroom closet. Gift-wrapped. The size of a large shoebox, or a small coffin.

LETTER TO READERS OF COSMO GIRL— "SKIN AND BONES"

DANNIAH DAHER, 14

TURKEY FOOT MIDDLE SCHOOL
EDGEWOOD, KY
TEACHER: MELANIE DULANEY

April 11, 2007

Dear Reader:

Imagine a young girl about 14. She leans over a toilet grasping her burning throat, tears trickling down her cheeks. She tries to throw up the salad she nibbled for lunch, but her mind is too tired; her body is too weak. Her stomach is empty, and her body is ill. The girl's mind turns fuzzy, and suddenly she collapses on the dirty tile floor. What would cause this kind of behavior? The answers lie within the fashion magazine the girl had been scrutinizing, now crumpled in the corner of the bathroom stall. Snapshots of glamorous models, all who seem to have the "perfect" lifestyle, fill the pages. When did size 6 become too fat? When did bulimia become the hottest trend? And the most misunderstood topic for young girls . . . Why has anorexia become attractive?

Overly thin models and celebrities are worshiped by the media. They affect our world by making anorexia look beautiful. The wrong message is getting out that girls need to be needle thin; these traits have been mistaken for "perfect." Girls have been wrongly taught by *US Weekly* and *Teen People* that beautiful is skinny, blond, and luxurious. Most teenage girls keep a radar on fashion magazines. When they flip through the pages of that glitzy magazine each day, what do they see? Super-skinny people who look like they have it all: beauty, fame, and money. It perplexes me that teens would want to look like Nicole Richie or Mary-Kate Olsen. But these sickly thin young ladies are constantly affecting the teenage world; it's hard not to notice them. Five million Americans live with eating disorders and thin celebs are the main reason girls fall into the clutches of super-skinniness syndrome.

Models are a big contributor to the super-skinny problem. They are, however, waking up a bit. Agencies like Ford Modeling Agency are starting to do something about their sickly thin, and sometimes anorexic, clients. Recently, designers in Spain suddenly chose to help the fight against anorexia. They imposed a minimum weight-to-height ratio on all their models after a model in Uruguay died from heart failure on the runway. Milan followed Spain's example, requiring that every catwalker present a "health" license.

But money is still the agencies' number one priority, and they aren't just going to dump their thinnest models, even if the models may be anorexic. Normally, the thinner a model is, the more successful she will be. Council of Fashion Designers of America president Diane von Furstenberg admitted in an interview, "The truth is, in order to be a model, you have to be skinny." She also stated, "When I cast [models] in my show, [being chubby or thin] is in the back of my mind." She also said, "We should be sensitive to this problem. We should promote health. I am all for empowering women, not treating them as pieces of meat!"

Losing a modeling career is not the worst consequence of anorexia. Death is very common. Anorexia recently claimed the life of a Brazilian model, supposedly dubbed "the next Gisele Bundchen."

Being too thin is VERY unhealthy, and statistics show people are the most vulnerable to anorexia after puberty. It's easy to get lost during our teenage years. Being a teen, you don't just have to deal with trying to stay healthy, but with trying to abstain from drugs, alcohol, and other bad influences. Girls I know talk about how fat they are, or how they are going to lose this much weight. I think it's a waste of time. Some girls may become anorexic without even trying; people who are depressed will sometimes not eat. Stress also leads to anorexia. Say a teen has busloads of homework, soccer practice, piano lessons, and on top of all that, lacks self-confidence and is insecure about her figure. This kind of hectic lifestyle can lead to serious medical problems like anorexia. An anorexic young woman is 12 times more likely to die than a woman her same age without an eating disorder. Anorexia strips years off your life and it weakens your heart and your body. But you can change your fate. Anorexia doesn't have to take over your life. You are in control.

Given all the risks teens face today, it's very likely that many girls and guys will have weight issues. While it is true that girls are more likely to become anorexic—95% of sufferers are female—guys should still stay on their toes. A decade or so ago, anorexia wasn't a big deal. Now that so many teens are getting stuck in the messy web of anorexia, statistics are not on our side. A lot of teenagers think being super-thin is beautiful, but beneath the skin and bones, anorexia and bulimia are very hideous. They are ugly killers. Remember this letter the next time you sit down for a meal, and please have a second serving.

Best Regards,
A Seventh Grader

DEAF AND—SMART?
RACHEL KOLB, 17
ALBUQUERQUE ACADEMY
ALBUQUERQUE, NM
TEACHER: CYNTHIA MOORE

I don't think I have ever been able to pinpoint the exact attitude I hold for my deafness. It has always simultaneously been a minor detail and an insurmountable obstacle. In one moment, I feel comforted to know that I have one distinguishing characteristic that will never change; in another, this very fact drives me to despair. Surpassing my ambivalence, however, is the belief that my deafness gives me a keener sense of motivation and identity than I might have had otherwise. Both these spurring forces prompt me to do well, but they often arise from the heels of discrimination or misconception.

One example of such a motivating discrimination, if that description makes sense, is the phrase "deaf and dumb." Despite the fact that my hearing loss bars me from overhearing others' conversations, the times I have stumbled across this phrase just might rival the number of entries in the dictionary. When I was young, merely reading it in a book could stir me to bewildered tears. I could not understand where such a label would come from, even less so why anyone would wish to apply it to me. Even now, my reaction is sometimes nearly as emotional. I disregard the common excuse that this phrase essentially arose from the stereotype that deaf people cannot speak (see "deaf—mute") and therefore are "dumb." Such attempted innocence provides no justification for its implications: that deaf people are somehow inferior in intelligence. I scarcely can believe that during an age when discrimination is routinely counseled against, this one could endure virtually unnoticed. This fact is distressing to me, and signifies more than mere unawareness. Though the deaf population perhaps has not spoken up for themselves as they should, there is no excuse for the continuing ignorance of the hearing population.

I cannot count how many people I have met who have some preconceived notion of deafness or seem determined to treat me a certain way despite the fact that they have never met anyone with my disability. Either they behave as if I were more or less than I am, or a perplexing combination of both. There are the ones who, at the moment they meet me and observe my communication skills—skills I have worked the span of my life to acquire, skills that a high percentile of deaf people never approach—they automatically assume that I can, therefore, understand every word they say. It comes to their mystification that I constantly ask for repetition and sometimes cannot maintain the regular conversation they expect without the aid of an interpreter. They have assumed my aptitude to be more than it is; I can only imagine their surprise if I told them that I only understand perhaps a third of what they say.

There are also the ones who never give me a chance to exhibit my skills and my intelligence before they dispense the judgment that I am physically, never mind mentally, incapable of accomplishing anything on my own. To these people deafness seems to be a retarding disability, and thus every blunder I make—real or imagined—must be tolerated with a nod, a sympathetic smile, and perhaps even a shoulder pat or two. Their problem is the opposite of the first group; while my disability makes those individuals uncomfortable to the point where they would rather pretend it does not exist, this latter faction is intrinsically focused on it and all but unable to look past it to my true capabilities. Thankfully most humans fall more toward the neutral zone between these two extremes, it is rare that I meet the individual who sees me as I am: not made of glass, but not completely independent either. These people, who choose not to view their world only from their limited outlook, are also the ones who often choose to pursue a deeper relationship with me, learning sign language and unabashedly asking questions that make many others uncomfortable (such as, "How much can you really hear with your hearing aids?"). They are the rare ones, and the ones whom I have learned to value and cherish.

For many, however, "deaf and dumb" is the reality. Although I have never come across anyone who purposefully insulted me with that stereotype, it is still used far too often for comfort. It is so prolific within books and movies—especially dated ones and so-called classics—that the mainstream public has ceased to notice its derogatory qualities, if they ever did to begin with. I still remember my explosive anger in tenth grade when being subjected to it time after time while reading *The Adventures of Huckleberry Finn*, where descriptions like "stupid and leather-headed" and saying "'goo—goo—goo—goo—goo' all the time, like a baby that can't talk" abound when referring to deaf people. Even more infuriating was the fact that none of my classmates seemed to regard such stereotypes as a matter of personal insult. They failed to comprehend the intense emotion that "deaf and dumb" arouses in me, rooting from the assumption that simply because a deaf person's capability to communicate normally is limited, they must possess an intellectual competence lesser than that of ordinary hearing people. Although I have met several deaf individuals who struggle in academic areas—especially language skills—they are not to blame for their difficulties. In truth there is no real culprit in such a situation, but if there were it would manifest in the form of the hearing culture that insists upon maintaining this stereotype with such aggravating nonchalance.

By this I fully mean to imply that the deaf children who are born to deaf parents are usually the fortunate ones. More often than not, the ones born to hearing parents are forced to suffer through the refusal of their family to learn to communicate. This is another saddening example of ignorance, and like most other ignorance, it stems from lack of education. However, in my mind its effects run so deep that the argument of mere personal delusion is not entirely justified. I have been fortunate enough to be born to parents who made every effort at providing me with a normal life from the time my disability became apparent, but despite their care, the outside world has seeped in. It is impossible for them, for anyone, to ensure that every word, every spoken facet that I burn to understand, is translated for me. From the curtain of incomprehension this ensures, I have learned one of my most vital and terrible lessons: a world in which one cannot communicate ranks among the worst of all punishments. With its accompanying frustrations, its silent moments of yearning to be understood, it is certainly one I would never bestow on my worst enemy. Yet I can do what most deaf people cannot. I can speak; I can lipread; I have mastered the written English language whose grammar varies so drastically from that of American Sign Language; in many cases, I can communicate to some extent. If a person with my scale of hearing loss could ever assimilate themselves completely into hearing culture, I have as good a shot at it as any.

From this statement I derive several conclusions that sear my soul. First of all, it makes me feel for those who have not been bestowed with the advantage of breaking free, if only partially, from the deaf world's narrow bounds. Second, I am not typical, and so the task of finding individuals who can relate to my struggle is often formidable. Third, the expectations others have of me as a deaf person are nearly always off the mark. I consider myself lucky to be differentiated from the majority of deaf children who end up separated from their families in state-sponsored institutes, but at the same time such a distinguishing factor can be very isolating.

When I think of this, I think of the frequent frustration of conversation with individuals who do not sign. I think of switching on the television to a particular program of interest, only to be immediately rejected from watching because its producers were not thoughtful enough to include closed captioning. I think of being unable to accomplish even small things, such as visits to the doctor, without the assistance of an interpreter. And I think of the bouts of paralyzing terror that come with the moments that I realize, this is the way it is, this is the way it will always be. I have always been stuck in the gap between two worlds, never able to put both feet on one side or the other. I think I have always realized this, but never as vividly as I did while attending a winter camp for the deaf three years ago.

Shortly after arrival on the first day, a small group of kids, including me, gathered around three or four high school seniors and initiated a tepid conversation. Not having the asset of previous introductions, our discussion soon steered to the common factor between us, our deafness. Out of the seven or eight present, maybe three had hearing aids, and only one had a cochlear implant. This boy in particular had been raised orally: that is, he leaned more toward the hard-of-hearing side of the hearing-loss spectrum, and thus had enough sensory ability to get along competently in the hearing world without the assistance of sign language. As a result, his signs were inaccurate and fumbling; the other kids latched on him right away and accused him of being lacking in "deaf pride."

Deaf pride? I watched in bewilderment as their flying hands condemned him an outcast, and though they did not turn on me that day, I realized that they might as well have condemned me too. It was then that I first understood that we, individuals supposedly unified by the pride of disability, were in fact worlds apart. Unable to handle their resentment toward the difficulty and misunderstanding of their lives in the hearing world, they had chosen to retreat within a hemisphere of deaf isolation. Although I knew such bitterness all too well, I had learned how to keep it on a short rein. I did not know what "deaf pride" was, had no personal sense or experience of it. All I knew, all I had ever known, was deaf shame.

I did not gain the opportunity to reflect on this until well after the camp had ended, and when I did, I felt torn between two worlds. This condition is one I have always struggled with as I attempt to live my life in the hearing world while inherently aware that I am deaf, but not until that point did I literally feel the discomfort of being shoved on the fence. The ideal I had clung to, perhaps foolishly, of a happier deaf existence was now permanently dented. I wondered where my piece belonged in life, if it fit into neither the deaf puzzle nor the hearing one. No distinct mold existed after which I could model myself, and so I was forced to realize that my existence is my own.

It is through this, oddly enough, that I gain my strength. Knowing that my identity does not tie into that of a larger group gives me a certain freedom that I imagine others do not have; on the other hand, I constantly find myself pressed to maintain my self-image against outside discriminations such as "deaf and dumb." This perhaps contributes to the queer perfectionist drive that has always lingered within me, the unshakable belief that because I enter others' subconscious as lesser, I must leave it as greater. Thus I believe that my deafness has directly influenced components that I value in myself, such as my work ethic. Who can say that I would be the same person were it not for this accident of nature? And while I may resent fate at times, how can I question it, how can I say that my life would be better if not for my disability? Perhaps in some ways it would be, but at the same time I would have lost an essential part of myself.

It is in this way that I must turn back to the chief source of my complaints, the hearing culture whose reality has been so difficult to equate with my ideals, but whose struggles have shaped my identity and given me a central purpose: to overcome misunderstanding. Yes, I am deaf. No, I can't say I'm proud of it, but I have no choice but to accept it. Yes, I would seize the opportunity to be a normal person in an instant. But since that will never happen, I might as well seize my lot not as a curse, but as an opportunity. The needling tension of living in a constantly misunderstanding world may always endure, but I have a choice of how to handle it. All deaf people, all disadvantaged people in general, make this choice every day. Some choose to view their situation as oppression and release their sentiments as bitterness.

I can view my situation as a lifelong challenge and consequently rise to the occasion. My goal: take charge of my old nemesis, my deafness, and move toward the day when the description "deaf and smart" will not be entirely unheard of.

REGRET #17 FROM ABIGAIL'S DIARY
ALLISON CUMMINGS, 18
SHELBY HIGH
SHELBY, NC
TEACHER: JASON LINEBERGER

now that i'm found
i don't miss the sex
that made me feel
wooden, hollow,
and rotten
after we lay concealed
in the hay that stank
gloriously of our sweat
and your horse's manure,

or your hands
that churned me hot
'til i became melted butter
to grease your rickety
rutting machinery
while you panted
"i love you" in steamy,
bland-tasting monotone,

nor swearing
myself into frenzy
with a bundle of promises
i never tied together

that broke easily,
like sticks gathered for firewood
when your twitching mouth
softened my resolve.

i miss fancying that,
had i told you my heart,
warm but fragmented,
was breaking like the morning rays
over your untended fields
each time i watched you,
reddened in the sunrise,
creep back to your wife,
you would have changed.

HATS
DANIEL ROSS, 14
HUNTER COLLEGE HIGH SCHOOL
NEW YORK, NY
TEACHER: NIKKI WEINSTEIN

Most of each day is spent
exchanging subtle, surreptitious
glances at each other's hats.
Maurice's, his is a peculiar asphalt color,
like an olive roasted slightly too long,
and we envy him for it. Mine is
far too tall to keep on straight, and frequently
slides to a jaunty angle. It is wider
than Maurice's,
which gives me pride, but it is also
crooked at the inseam and too small
to encompass my entire head.
The man who directs all that we do
never removes his hat; we don't blame him.
We would enjoy it, too, if one of us had a hat
like that, so wide-brimmed, so flat, so black
it seems almost to bleed into the walls
like ink pressed too long against a page. Most
of our acquaintances from the room two doors over
have hats of a greenish color, which might be
suitable for them,
but in all honesty
we couldn't imagine
having to wear one of *those* all day.

THE GENERAL STORE

JESSI GLUECK, 12

LEAWOOD MIDDLE SCHOOL
LEAWOOD, KS
TEACHER: AMANDA WITTY

It was summer, the summer of 1935. It was one of the hottest summers that the small Midwestern town had ever seen. The grass and the road were both baked so yellow that you couldn't tell where Main Street ended and the lawns of the little houses began.

Even so, no one was really worried about the weather. It was not a town where worrying came easily. It was the kind of place where people sat on their porches and drank lemonade in the evening, smelling the richly flower-scented breezes and chatting of this and that. It was a town where children would play street-wide games of basketball and kick-the-can and hold races at the community pool. It was the sort of place that is lost today, where no one was rich and no one was poor and almost everyone was happy.

In this town and in this world there lived a 12-year-old boy with unruly red hair and deep brown eyes. He didn't really like school or basketball or kick-the-can or swimming. He wasn't very good at anything in particular, and though he was liked well enough, he didn't have very many close friends. None of this seemed to bother him, though; he quietly and contentedly lived out a very ordinary existence, and never did anything to set himself apart.

But one day that summer, he did something almost unheard of for a 12-year-old boy in that sort of town. He did it quietly, deliberately, and without any show, as he did everything. He applied for a job at the General Store, and got it.

This caused a stir among his peers. They accosted him as he made his way down the dusty path to the store, shouting questions: "Whaddaya wanna work for, anyway?" "Are ya gettin paid?" "How much?" He answered them, calmly, and they learned that he was getting paid, but hardly anything at all. He told them that he wanted to work because he liked the General Store, a response that baffled them so much that they left him to discuss it. They could not understand that a boy their age would abandon a summer full of games and swimming to work at the General Store just because he liked the place. In fact, they were a little disgusted with him.

This response bothered the boy not at all. He had first entered the General Store when he was, he considered, a mere child of six years old, and it had been his favorite place in the world ever since. He loved the coffee smell, the silky stacks of ribbons and cloth, the boxes and bags and barrels of everything under the sun. It was dusty and cool inside, but the windows were always kept crystal clear and free of all fingerprints, so that the sunlight could filter in and create little pools of warmth at the front of the shop.

The boy was fond of everything about this place, and so he had overcome a little shyness and marched in and asked if the shopkeeper needed any help. The old man with the fuzz of white hair around his temples gave him a crinkled smile and said yes, he could use some help, and would be glad to let the boy clean up around the store and perhaps talk to the customers to convince them to buy things. He would even pay him a little. The boy left the store walking on air. He wanted to shout and yell and jump and dance, but in his peculiar, self-contained way, he merely whistled merrily and smiled broadly at the world in general.

The next morning he rose early and washed his face. He wanted to look especially neat for his first day at the store. Then he walked happily along the path from his home to the shop, feeling the cool of the trees' shadows and the warmth of sunshine that had not yet become searing. He pushed open the door of the General Store and let the quiet and the musty smell wash over him. It was so silent that at first he thought he had arrived before the shopkeeper. Then he saw the old man, who was sitting in front of the window and watching the street outside. It was deserted at this hour, and very peaceful, with the old oaks and the little storefronts outlined in gold light and the street striped with blue shadows.

"Good morning, sir," said the boy, after filling his eyes with the calming sight. "Good morning," said the old man. "Well, we'd best get started, hadn't we?"

"Yes, sir."

The boy began his first day at work by dusting all the shelves and sweeping a mop across the floors. The tasks were mundane, but the boy was happy in his work, and he handled everything from mop to bucket to the items on the shelves with exquisite care. The shopkeeper smiled as he watched the boy delicately swipe the feather duster across a shelf, not even flinching when a bit of dust got in his eyes. He worked quickly and the store was more than presentable when the first customer arrived.

The first customer was a lady, a little stooped and very careworn, but with a mouth that curved up at the corners. She seemed cheerful enough, and the boy was not nervous when the shopkeeper nodded at him to go to the door and welcome her.

"Hello," said the boy with a smile. "Fine morning, isn't it? Well, what are you looking to buy today?" After this little speech, the boy felt like clapping a hand over his mouth. Where had all these words come from? He had never talked to a stranger before, and he had not given a thought to what he would say if invited to address a customer. The words seemed to have been born somewhere in his subconscious and they jumped into his head just when they were needed.

The lady was charmed. "Well," she began, "I need some cloth . . . yes, plenty of cloth . . . and some soap, and flour, and whatever fruit is in season. Oh, and, of course, my husband will be wanting his coffee."

Delighted with this order, the boy showed her around the store, talking about each of the items in turn, not knowing where these words came from, either, but saying them anyway. He spoke simply, some-times telling stories about how his own mother used materials at home, or the dress that his little sister had worn to school, or the look on his father's face as he tasted freshly-brewed coffee in the morning. Sometimes he encouraged her to feel, and taste, and sniff, believing that the scents and sights and textures that had filled his head since he was six could not fail to please her. All of it was unpretentious, earnest, and enjoyable to both parties, and the lady finally left after an hour with more goods than her sack could hold and a smile lighting her face.

The boy heard a sound as the door closed behind her. He turned. It was the shopkeeper. He was applauding. The boy shuffled his feet, vastly pleased but a little embarrassed. The shopkeeper stopped clap-ping and came around the counter to put his hand on the boy's shoul-der. For a few moments he did not speak, and when the boy looked up questioningly, he could see tears sparkling in the bright green eyes. Finally the shopkeeper swallowed, and said very quietly, "Well done. Very well done. You . . ." he stopped. He took his hand off the boy's shoulder and went back behind the counter, smiling out at the street as it filled with the bustle of a new day.

What remained of the morning fled by into afternoon and evening, and the boy helped every customer and enjoyed himself more each time. At 7:00, the shopkeeper told the boy to go home, reminding him that he had not eaten all day, and that his parents would be won-dering what had become of him. In response to this, the boy took his pay and bought a small pie and a sandwich at the diner across the street. Then he ran all the way home, informed his parents that he'd be back late, and ate his food on a bench outside the General Store, letting the delicious breezes wash over him.

He was back in the store by 7:45. The shopkeeper laughed, threw up his hands, and let the boy go back to greeting the customers.

The store was shut up by 10:00 and the boy walked slowly home, savoring the memories of the wonderful day. He took a stroll around the house in the quiet, fragrant night, and then climbed the steps and walked to his room. He rolled himself in a blanket and fell into the best sleep he could ever remember, the sleep of one who is truly content.

The next day was the same, and the next day, and the day after that. And so the summer wore away, a blissfully happy time for the boy. Ever so gradually, the days began to shorten, and the nights to grow imperceptibly cooler and longer, and before the boy had a chance to think about it, school was starting again. He ached with sadness when he thought about the mornings and early afternoons he was missing at the store, the hushed calm at dawn and the steady bustle from noon to 2:00. But by 2:30, he was there, charming the customers with his ever-present effervescence and sincerity. No matter what happened at school, in the shop he was always smiling. He couldn't help it. It was his home.

The months of the school year began to slip by. The rainy warmth of September was followed by the sharp chill and brilliant leaves of October, and then the snow came, thick and powdery, and holiday time and Christmas carols. Then the snow began to melt, and the earth glided into a cool and lovely spring. And then it was summer again, and the boy had never stopped working at the shop.

Summer after summer, year after year passed like this. The boy grew taller and stronger and his hair stuck up even more. He grew better at arithmetic and started spending more time behind the counter at the General Store, often totaling the customers' money in his head. But he never stopped talking to people, never stopped smiling, and never stopped telling stories of his own family and how they used the good products sold at the store.

Meanwhile, in the world beyond the small town, destinies were shifting. War was coming. Papers began to talk about places with unpronounceable names. Even little villages like the boy's could not be oblivious. In 1940, men in the town started going off to join the Army. It made the boy's stomach turn over to think about his friends fighting and being killed in strange lands far away.

But there was the shop to tend to and the old shopkeeper, who was very old now, to think of, and inevitably when he started considering whether he would join the war, his mind was grasped by other things.

Then, on December 7, 1941, America was rocked to its foundations by Pearl Harbor. The boy kept looking at the photographs in the paper and alternately wanted to cry and rage. How did these foreign men rationalize killing innocent people? What did they know of the beauty of this country, of the peace to be found here? The United States of America must not stand for this. The boy could not stand for this. His 18th birthday was in January. On that day, he would enlist.

And then, unbelievably, his world was laid in ruins again. The shopkeeper died on December 19.

The funeral had no meaning for the boy. He stood, shivering, miserable, as the pastor said prayers and people made long, empty speeches. His tears froze on his cheeks and his ears throbbed with pain and sadness. He kept seeing the shopkeeper as he had on his first day working at the shop, with tears sparkling in his wise old eyes and his strong yet gentle hand on the boy's shoulder.

The old man had no living relatives and he left the shop to the boy. But now—now, the boy did not want it. For the first time, the neatly organized shelves and sparkling windows seemed bare to him. He ran the shop listlessly until his birthday, and then he packed up and left to join the Army, with no show or ceremony, just as he'd always done everything. His parents and sister cried, but he had already sobbed himself dry.

He went off to war. Four long, cold, gray years passed, years when there was never enough food and never enough sleep and never enough happiness. The boy made friends and watched them die, he learned to kill without crying, and all the while, the only thing he could think of was the little General Store back home, waiting for him. In this state of sadness and hardship, the boy slowly learned to be a man.

Then, one glorious day in 1945, it was over, it was all over. The young man remembered, as he walked the streets of the summer-filled town for the first time since the war, what it was he had been fighting for.

He was welcomed home with open arms and tears and banners and the high school marching band. He was celebrating, too. At last, after four years of battle within himself and against the enemy, the pain of the deaths of his friends and of the shopkeeper began to dull. The man understood, deep within himself, that the only thing to do now was to go back to the store and work hard to make the customers happy, just as the old shopkeeper had done. And so he went. Everything was back to normal.

And yet—things were not quite normal. He had returned to a changed world, or perhaps it had not yet changed, but it was on the brink of change. The man held on to his one little piece of the past, running the store as it had always been run and was meant to be run. But the years kept ticking inexorably by, and the view from the shop's window began to reflect the changes rocking the world.

First, the cars came. They filled the quiet little Main Street with smoke and noise and fumes, crashing about at ungodly hours of the day and night. The man never again saw a peaceful early morning like the one when he first started working at the shop. Then, the clothing began to change, girls wearing pants and skirts well above the knee, men wearing cotton T-shirts. The protesters and hippies arrived, with horrible alcohol and drugs and cigarettes that filled the air with acrid smoke. They stood in the town square sometimes, holding signs that didn't make sense to the man. The town seemed to be growing by leaps and bounds. It made the man very sad, the day he realized that he didn't know the name of everyone who lived there anymore.

Still, he kept working, speaking gently to his customers about his childhood and any good or enjoyable times during the war. And, despite all the change, the customers kept coming, and left the store with smiles on their faces and warmth in their hearts.

The hippies melted away and a Wal-Mart was established up the street. Sometimes he would see customers standing on the sidewalk nearby, glancing from the General Store to the Wal-Mart and often scurrying guiltily into the big, new, gleaming block of white concrete. But there were still those who knew better, and kept coming to the little shop. Though much had changed, people still loved the quiet and the big, clear windows and the way the man behind the counter would talk to them in his earnest, sparkling voice.

And then, the new millennium arrived with great bustle and celebration. It was a new age. So much was different. So much had changed for the worse. The man was beginning to feel a great heaviness in his heart. He was starting to wonder if he wanted to run the store anymore. The people were impatient, even angry. No one had time to talk; no one had time to listen. This new generation was strange and heartbreaking to him. As the years passed, he knew he must soon retire.

One cold day in 2007, he made up his mind for sure. He began pulling things down from the shelves, boxing them, but then stopped, a great lump in his throat. He looked out the window and caught a glimpse of his own reflection: a wrinkled, stooped old man with a fuzz of white hair around his temples. He looked spent and withered. He glanced out at the street, full of asphalt and cars and towering buildings. His time had passed. He felt very sad and very alone.

And then a boy came through the door, very small and with large blue eyes, and looked up at the old shopkeeper.

"Do you need any help around here?" he asked timidly.

For a moment, the man could not speak. Then warmth welled up within him, and words came. "Yes," he said softly, "I could use some help. I'd be glad to let you clean up around the store and perhaps talk to the customers to convince them to buy things. I'll even pay you a little."

"Oh, thank you, sir!" said the boy, and then he walked out of the shop, whistling.

OSTRICHES
SHARON JAN, 15

ORANGE COUNTY HIGH SCHOOL OF THE ARTS
SANTA ANA, CA
TEACHER: JENNIFER CARR

HIM

Like ostriches that ignore danger to escape it, it seems that everybody in the world has their head shoved in the ground. And if somebody were to pull them out and try and get them to face the problem, they would squawk, "Idiot! Now it can see us!"

I guess they don't realize how fat their pink, feathery butts are.

I don't want to be stuck around all these ostriches or, even worse, be one of them. I wish that not just their heads but all of them would disappear all the way into the dirt. And yet the bodies extending from their necks are still swaying aboveground, shaking from the cold, or maybe it's fear.

You can never get away from the ostriches.

I've learned that you can tell a lot about a person by the way he drinks his tea. Like somebody with an itching heart gulping frantically, his spit and the brown liquid running down his chin. Or a restless kid gurgling the hot tea in his mouth, swishing it behind his teeth and under his tongue—that kind of thing.

She holds the cracked cup like she's freezing, and the way the tea slides down her throat makes me want to cry.

HER

My grandmother lay on her ragged futon, her face more deflated than its quilted surface. She told me, "The lightning in the wind has turned into wolves, and you are pressed in the lee of a stone wall. And look! Are you going to make an imprint in the bricks? Will you show the world what you are?"

"That's not a proverb, sobe," I said to her.

Then she died.

What are you supposed to do with yourself when somebody's dying words are still hanging on your tail like that? I resolve that if I die it will be inside a tree or somewhere just as hidden and I won't say a word to anyone, not even the insects.

It is the spring of 1955, and still I have not forgotten.

As I drink my tea I wonder how a hibakusha, a survivor, lives. Is it even a hibakusha's responsibility to live? Does surviving require living? I hope not, or I may never die.

As I think this, he comes to sit next to me, bowing furiously. He smiles sheepishly, his crooked teeth pushing against the lopsided curve of his lips. His hair is cropped short, but he slouches as if he is still waiting for bangs to fall over his eyes. I smile.

But I can't do that. How can I live happily when so many others have died? I can't be content without honoring the deceased. If I am, all I see are hands stretched across collapsed walls, eyes melting in their sockets. And everywhere there are burning buildings that should be long destroyed and gone and a thousand cranes flung aloft in the light.

HIM

Why is it that I can only see the eyes of ostriches, even when their heads are stuck in the ground? What about the eyes that I really want to see? She is looking to a world I don't know and can't guess. I won't guess—

I first heard about the bombing of Hiroshima when my father read about it to us from the newspaper over dinner. My mother clucked and put more eel in my father's bowl. But I wondered if people were tearing their hair and breathing last breaths at that moment. That night, the air felt heavy with wails.

People still talk about the H-bomb, and the hibakusha who felt its touch. Even now, the time and site of the destruction are on the tongues of everyone who lived to experience it. There are those who talk about the bomb as if it were holy lightning falling from heaven. Like God's black hands, they say, descending to earth in a swift motion to fall upon His subjects. I don't think the hibakusha really believe this, but they still hang onto this hopeful divine right with an offhand wistfulness. I suppose it's easier to be unnatural when you can at least think that you are part of a chosen people—

No, I won't guess.

She asks me if I've ever made a thousand origami cranes. Folding a thousand cranes within one year is supposed to bring good fortune to the maker, especially healing to a disease. I'm afraid to tell her, but I can't even fold cranes. I tried and failed miserably when I was a child, and haven't revived the attempt since then. I remind myself to ask my mother to teach me one more time.

I think I will tell her how beautiful her hands are once I fold a thousand cranes.

No, that'll take too long. Maybe just a hundred.

Or five.

Her

When we finish our tea, he offers to take me home. As I walk with him down the road, I can't help wondering if I'm even allowed to stand next to him. What if one of the girls who died looked upon him, loved him? I wonder if this would count as dishonoring the dead.

I hear my father in my head, speaking loudly as he did when his friends came over to talk of politics over sake. "You've got to take what you want and no questions about it! Nobody's doing anybody any favors. Wife, the bottle!"

Sake only tastes good when you want something.

I think about Grandmother. I try to reconstruct the talk she had with me before she died. I imagine that what she really said was, "What happens happens, and you must only think of yourself. Don't let guilt take you. Live a full life—I allow you to."

Then I would have said, "Yes, sobe. Thank you so much."

If that was how it had happened, I'd be able to burn incense sticks for Grandmother without hurling them to the ground.

When we reach my home, I thank him. I hold out my hand to shake, but he takes it with his two hands.

Then.

He.

Says.

HIM

," I say.

Or do I? Funny how when important things happen they seem to haze around the corners and make you dizzy, like at this moment when she looks at me (at me!), and I think that this could all end up like in those nice Western fairy tales, living, happily, ever after, and then she smiles, at least I think she does, oh I do hope she did, so I try to hold her to me, or at least touch her hand to my face, but then I look at her again and her eyes are far away, they are like ostrich eyes, but I don't want her to be an ostrich, and she is holding a rock, she is throwing a rock, she is throwing at me, she says get out, she screams, don't touch me, she cries, there is lightning on her back, there is fire in her face, so I run like a dog with no tail, that bare, and when I am almost too far away to hear she says sorry, but I keep running because I don't think I am supposed to look back.

HER

August 6, 1945

The world has finally imploded into fire, or maybe it is that fire has evolved and caught the world, I thought. It seemed as if nothing stood still, even in the muggy summer. I felt the dark pressure of every building folding and compressing into the ground. This turmoil came in a sheet of white sun covering the sky that swooped down to catch us in its burnt claws.

That summer Minami finished making her one thousand paper cranes. We couldn't afford so much origami paper, so she folded them out of squares from scraps of old newspapers and discarded flyers. She put them in a large jar and kept them where everybody could see. "I made them for Grandmother, so that she can come out of the hospital," she said, but now I think it would have been better if she had saved them for herself.

On that day, I saw the ugliness of myself. It was in the wide eyes of the people scattered about the ground. Their skin was peeling, dangling from their fingertips. A woman lay facedown in the earth, her kimono wrapped loosely around her. The parts of her back that were exposed were burned in the pattern of the kimono's cloth. As I ran, I could feel the limbs of the dead people under me slipping, sometimes making me trip. I imagined what would happen if their blood spurted out and touched me. I thought that the blood would not slide down or dry, but be absorbed by me. I felt like I was swelling up, becoming bloated with so many potential lives that were now wasted. Was I nothing but a sponge, fat with excess living discarded by the spirits?

That day should have been a story of bravery. It should have been me uniting with the other people against our common enemy, making a noble war. But I don't know what to do when I can't see an enemy, and the dead people I stepped on could not fight.

I saw my classmate under a collapsed wall. "Help," she croaked. She spoke like she had no words. I looked away and pretended not to have heard. She will die soon anyway, I told myself. And I have to save myself. I have to find my sister; I have to find Minami. But all I saw was myself reflected ugly in my classmate's eyes. I kept running.

What must the people who dropped the bomb have been thinking at that time? Yes, look at that. They crumple like insects. See, there's another one. Oh, this hot air is killing me! Nothing like genocide to work up a thirst.

I was so thirsty. The black rain began to fall.

HIM

As I walk across the bridge to get to my house, I watch the sunset disappear in the ripples of the water. The river underneath the bridge has swelled from the spring rains and burbles quietly as it runs over unseen pebbles and debris.

I finish crossing the bridge and begin down an avenue to reach the house where I board. This avenue is a busy one; small shops and stalls selling mochi and octopus balls line the street. Schoolgirls with hair cropped short giggle at the monkey-eared boys who follow them, swinging brown schoolbags behind them. At the end of the avenue is a tired tree sloping over the stalls and shops. Lovers pick flowers from it to slip in each other's hair and children swing from its branches, eating mochi stuffed with sweet red beans, their hands white and sticky.

HER

As I sleep, the world implodes to nothing, and fire blows thick and heavy. The lightning in the wind has turned into wolves, and I am pressed in the lee of a stone wall. When the wind quiets, I look back at the wall.

Grandma says, "There, that is your imprint in the bricks. That is your impact."

"But it is so small," I say. "It looks like a baby curled inside its mother's belly. See, I could fit that little dent in the wall inside my hand."

Grandma speaks. But the wind is snarling again, and I only hear snatches of what she says.

Pressed. Everybody. Bigger.

"What?" The wind blows loud.

Live. Long.

"I will, grandmother."

No. I. Live. Long.

"Yes, you did."

No. Want. Live. Long.

"But you did live long, sobe."

But. Did. They?

"Sobe?"

HIM

I sit in the shadow of the wall encircling the high school I had gone to, trying to remember how to fold the crane. A diagonal or horizontal fold? As I bend the final spike into a beak, she appears to me. She asks me, "If I tell you, will you listen? Will I be able to look at myself?" I don't know what she's saying, but her shoulders seem so weak at that moment that I give her the new crane, thinking that this is a 'yes'.

HER

August 8, 1945

Makeshift medical centers had begun to appear. People swathed in dirty bandages lay in tight rows. Some patients were so swollen they looked more like a caricature than the real person. Their puffy flesh peeked out from under too-tight bandages, pale and veiny. The medical station was where I found Minami. I could barely recognize her beneath the dirty bindings. A fly landed between her cracked lips. The insects realized what I could not say. I spoke to Minami nervously.

"Don't worry, we'll get out of this."

"We'll be fine. We'll be together to see New Year's."

"Remember the fireworks?"

"You'll be alright soon—the doctors will take care of you."

"Oh God, I don't know what to do."

"Please, open your eyes. Get up. Help me."

"I'm tired."

When I woke up, I knew that my sister would not live. It was too terrible to see unknown people cover her face with a dirty cloth, so I left. I told her I was sorry.

After walking so long, I found myself at the doorstep of my mutilated home. I walked inside. There it sat, Minami's jar of a thousand cranes, unbroken. The roof had all but caved in, the walls were splintered and peeling, and the world had been reduced to ashes. But the cranes had survived. Then where was the good luck, the healing they should have brought? Where was Minami? The room blurred. It was not fair that the thousand cranes should live and she should die.

They would not live.

They would die.

August 9, 1945

I burned the cranes. They folded and curled miserably in the fire, shrinking into black. The words on their newspaper wings seemed to detach themselves before disappearing. It was like a final effort from the immobile birds to fly, or live somehow. This is what burning luck looks like, I thought. The ink mixed with smoke rose heavily into the air, floating upwards until the wind blew it apart.

HIM

What would happen if I were to spend the rest of my life with her? I don't know if we could ever look and not see the bomb. I don't know if she would even always be there, or if I would glance next to me one day to find that she had gone. But it is good to tell of the things that have happened, just as it is good to look at danger, even if it comes as a black barrier that does not move. I suppose everybody can be an ostrich without knowing it, but at least we have found ourselves out.

HER

I think I know what Grandma meant now when she said the thing in my dream that I could not hear. It is that when all of those hibakusha in Hiroshima are pressed against the wall—when everybody pushes— our imprint will be larger, one that anybody could see. My tiny fetus-dent in the bricks will grow with every person who presses himself or herself against the wolves in the wind and straighten to a baby learning to walk. So long after Hiroshima fell to its knees, we will be taking our first steps.

JINGLE BEARS AND RAW SQUID
YUMI SHIROMA, 13

THE MASTERS SCHOOL
DOBBS FERRY, NY
TEACHER: MARK FRIEDMAN

The Japanese don't believe in many things. Beds, for one. Most people sleep on mattresses on the floor that they can fold up and tuck away in a closet in the morning, out of sheer lack of space. One main room often has to serve as kitchen, living room, and bedroom for an entire family.

Some other things in which they generally don't believe are pierced ears, crime and cooked food. And they don't believe in chocolate ice cream, at least not in Tokyo.

They do believe in squid. Raw squid. And horses. Also raw, and served with soy sauce and a dandelion blossom.

More about that later.

Our story begins on a summer's day in northern Japan, as cold air sweeps in from a nearby mountain range.

■

"I've never seen such a big crab in my life." I point my small digital camera at the fish tank. The monstrous crustacean inside waves its legs irritably as the flash goes off. Short brown bristles cover its entire body. If only they were clustered more closely together, it might be mistaken for an oddly-hued, misshapen, and oversized toothbrush.

It's strange, though not quite as strange as the carousel for drying fish filets that I saw back in the town before this one. Pieces of salmon, about six inches long each, were clipped to a spinning structure powered by electricity, set up outside a seafood store. If they were still alive, I would have said that they must be getting dizzy.

Now, my mother and I stand in a lodge of sorts at the start of the hiking trail leading up into the Daisetsuzan mountains. My dad should be buying some food to take up with us, but I can see him off to the side trying on what could very well be about to become the latest addition to his gallery of baseball caps: a yellow hat spoofing the Puma logo, with a picture of a bear and the word 'KUMA' embroidered in black. Kuma, or bear, is one of the few Japanese words I've picked up, mainly because bears are so common in this part of the country, and if I get eaten by one, I at least want to be able to identify it in the proper language.

The stall next to the hats sells bear bells. Supposedly, if you hang a bell somewhere on your person, the noise will scare off the large population of brown bears that lives in the mountains. However, from what I can see of the trail, it's so packed with tourists that no sane bear would come anywhere near it anyway.

My eyes wander to the left and come to rest on an incongruous little stall in the corner. "Can I get a snack?" I ask.

"Sure," my mom says. "Have a raw octopus tentacle? You used to teethe on these when you were a baby." She holds up a plastic bag filled with something rubbery and purple and covered in suction cups.

"No thank you. How about some ice cream? It looks like they have chocolate!"

This vacation has become a never-ending search for chocolate ice cream. You'd think that somewhere in the populous city of Tokyo there would be just one store that sold it, but no. They all have vanilla, red bean, green tea, coffee, strawberry, mint, a flavor called "pink" (but only when you're in a lily park), and no chocolate. I came close when we met the British yacht crew in Sapporo and helped them find an ATM in a 7-Eleven. Instead of an ATM, I found a Fudgesicle, but it just wasn't the same.

This stall, however, shows promise. Virtually all the ice cream vendors in Japan display two-foot-tall plastic ice cream cones outside their stores. These people have spray painted theirs black. So what if chocolate should be brown? Maybe they just didn't have the exact right shade of paint.

We walk over to the stall. Oddly enough, a picture of a squid decorates the flavor list. Well, I suppose it is a town famous for its squid fishing industry. I turn to my mom. "Can you read me that sign?" I ask, displaying my blissful ignorance of Japanese characters.

"Vanilla. Red bean. Green tea. Coffee. Strawberry. Mint. Um . . . "

That's six out of the seven flavors. "Chocolate?" I prompt.

"Ika-something . . . ikasumi? That can't be right . . . "

"Ikasumi!? As in . . . squid ink? Squid ink ice cream?"

This is another of the Japanese phrases in my vocabulary, due to an unpleasant experience in the Hakodate morning market, slightly past the fish carousel. A huge tank full of small squid stood in the center of the market, and the owners let tourists pay to get a fishing rod and a bucket and catch one. What they don't tell you—or, to be perfectly fair to the proprietors, what I didn't bother to ask my dad to translate—is that if you grab the squid by its body, it will ink you. I snagged a particularly agile one on my first try. It proceeded to flail around like a cephalopod with its head cut off, swinging around and around my head on the fishing pole and providing a great spectacle for the other tourists sitting on the nearby benches with camcorders. I finally grabbed it when it swung around in front of me for the fourth time. I received a complimentary and unexpected face full of squid ink as the mortified owner ran up to us with a dishcloth screaming, "Ikasumi! Ikasumi! Gomennasai, gomennasai!"

I shake my head to clear it of this unpleasant remembrance. "Never mind. I'm not so hungry after all."

■

Before today, I'd never been on top of a mountain and inside a cloud. It's not as wet as one might expect, just vaguely foggy, which seriously restricts visibility. We're not even at the highest peak yet; Mom and I have stopped to rest while my dad continues up to the top with his two Nikon cameras, one of normal size and another with a foot-long lens for photographing small objects, which I call The Bazooka. That's the last thing I'd want to lug up and down a mountain.

I'm slowly but surely starving. You'd be amazed how effectively raw squid can deter a person from eating. Lack of food eventually takes its toll, though. I have some gum, a plastic-wrapped sembei cracker, a box of BEAR caramels, and a box of BEER caramels in my shoulder bag, but none of these are particularly nourishing. I've also packed my notebook, a pencil, some embroidery thread that I've been using to weave bracelets, and a science fiction story magazine. I've already used the notebook to write down a description of this epic-looking mountain range, complete with sulfur-spewing fumaroles, scraggly bushes, and wild beasts, which will later go on to become the Dwarf homeworld in my novel. The book I started reading yesterday is unfortunately absent, due to its 1,123-page, dictionary-worthy length. I would go so far as to call it the second-to-last thing I'd want to lug up and down a mountain, despite my burning need to find out what happens to Paksenarrion after she's accepted into Duke Halveric's mercenary company. Perhaps there's something to be said for short stories after all.

I take out the bear caramels. I'm reasonably sure that they've never touched any seafood products in their lives, though I wouldn't be surprised if they turned out to be flavored with bear fat or something. But since I now know for sure that the beer caramels contain actual beer, from the Sapporo Beer Garden, I'm willing to take a chance.

I chew and swallow. It tastes almost normal, but the energy from one caramel won't last for very long. My dad had better finish his photo shoot soon so we can start heading back down these Dwarfish slopes and toward the hotel, and (hopefully) a nice, cooked meal.

Meanwhile, I can sit on a sun-warmed rock and watch all the clumsy tourists trip on the tiny loose stones littering the trail and go sliding down on their behinds. With their bear bells clinking, they look and sound like a herd of cows. Who needs TV for entertainment when you have this?

■

It takes My Honored Father the Bazooka Photographer another hour to get back. By now the sun is beginning to slip down the horizon like a huge, greasy egg yolk sliding down a blue ceramic plate. (Everything starts to look like food eventually, when you're hungry enough.) Most of the herds of tourists have cleared out by now, casting the trail into an eerie silence. If I were a bear and I wanted to go on a hike and watch the sunset, this is undoubtedly the time I would pick.

"Maybe we should have gotten one of those bear bells . . . " I say uneasily. My voice echoes off the mountain peaks.

Neither of my parents reply.

"Maybe we should try to make some noise just in case," I add.

Then I hear a sound coming from about a yard behind me. Not a growling bear, but something that sounds vaguely similar. A guttural voice half-mutters, half-sings, "Jingle bells, jingle bells . . . "

My father breaks off mid-verse. Having been raised in rural Japan, he never had cause to learn the all words to an American Christmas carol.

"Jingle all the way!" I supply. "And I hope I won't get eaten by a bear toda-ay!"

By the time we reach the bottom of the trail, we've gone through our entire repertoire of bear-, bell-, or mountain-related songs, including my personal favorite, a three-part round of "Benjie Met the Bear": Benjie met the bear, the bear met Benjie, the bear was bulgy, the bulge was Benjie . . .

My good mood lasts until we reach the hotel lobby, at which point it promptly evaporates when I find out that they're serving raw squid noodles and scallops as their main entree today. Tomorrow's shinkansen train back to the relative normality of Tokyo can't come soon enough.

SPECIAL THANKS

25,000 DEDICATED TEACHERS for motivating their students to participate in The Scholastic Art & Writing Awards.

81 REGIONAL AFFILIATES for uniting communities to celebrate creative youth.

LOCAL AND NATIONAL JURORS for lending their time and energy to emerging artists and writers.

JOYCE MAYNARD (ALUMNA, 1966, 1967, 1968, 1970 AND 1971) for continuing to give back to the Alliance and The Awards

PHILIP PEARLSTEIN (ALUMNUS, 1941 AND 1942) for inspiring young artists to follow in his footsteps.

STEVE DIAMOND (ALUMNUS, 1971) for his unwavering commitment to the Alliance for Young Artists & Writers.

TEMNETE SEBHATU for her tireless work on this anthology.

KENT WILLIAMSON for spreading the message to English and Language Arts teachers.

CHUCK PALAHNIUK for his fierce wit and unforgettable words of encouragement.

ABOUT THE AUTHORS

DINA ABDULHADI is from Alpharetta, GA, and makes amazing grilled cheese sandwiches (imagine thick slabs of cheese, slices of fresh tomato, and heavy, buttered bread). When she's not writing she can be found making art and thinking about validation from The System.

PAULA ALBANEZE lives in Honolulu, HI. She will be a 12th grader at Moanalua High in Honolulu, HI. Her fantasy short story titled *Sheol* is an existential exploration of morality set in the afterlife.

ALLEN BUTT is a native of Beaufort, SC. He writes because "when you sit down with Shakespeare or Cervantes or Joyce, you ask yourself, 'Do I have anything to add?' and as long as the answer keeps coming back as 'probably,' you keep on plugging." Allen will attend Presbyterian College in Clinton, SC, next year and plans to major in English.

SARAH CARNICK was born in South Bend, IN, but now lives in Simpsonville, SC. She can be found invariably reading or writing, and hopes to continue both in either New York or LA. A tick in the back of her head commands her to write.

AVITAL CHIZHIK is from Highland Park, NJ. Without her sophomore English teacher Mrs. Schachmovitz's urging, her writing would still be locked away in a diary. Her writing is informed by Nicole Krauss, Jonathan Safran Foer, Tolstoy, and Turgenev, and inspired by, among other things, the stories passed down by family members, foreign films, people in the street, renaissance art, and violins.

VICTORIA COLE is from Columbia, SC. She graduated from South Carolina Governor's School. Her writing shows a strong inclination toward the past, and a fixation on memory, writing things down, and taking photographs.

ELIZABETH COZART lives in Denver, IA, in a house "surrounded by cornfields." In ten years she sees herself "in a white lab coat and stethoscope, jabbing some poor fellow in the arm with a needle." Elizabeth will be attending Swarthmore College in Pennsylvania, where she plans to study biology and biochemistry, and would like to thank her parents for paying all of her outstanding library fines.

ALLISON CUMMINGS lives in Shelby, NC. She graduated from Shelby High School.

DANNIAH DAHER lives in Edgewood, KY. She plays soccer almost every day and is inspired by a very special writer: her mother. The simple thrill of writing a story is enough to keep her going. She looks forward to the challenge of translating an experience to the page. Danniah hopes to study literature in college.

MATTHEW JOSEPH DISLER lives in Richmond, VA. He has been playing both the piano and the alto saxophone since the age of nine, plays tennis and soccer, and is an amateur filmmaker. In ten years he sees himself studying either the arts or international relations in graduate school.

KATIE EISENBERG lives in Greenwich, CT. In her Personal Essay "*A, B, C, D, S, E, X,*" Katie learns about the birds and the bees a couple of years too early when she accidentally reads her parents' copy of the kama sutra. She graduated from Convent of the Sacred Heart.

JESSI GLUECK lives in Leawood, KS. Aside from writing, she feeds her interest in nature by maintaining a subscription to *National Geographic* and enjoys playing basketball. Jessi's poetry is inspired by the natural world but her works of fiction are informed by her fascination with relationships, the passage of time, and "the ways we change and the ways we stay the same." As a seventh grader, college is a long way away for Jessi, but she hopes to attend Harvard and study literature.

AIDAN Q. GRAHAM hails from Brooklyn, NY, a borough that has "spirit, passion, and most importantly, diversity." When he's not writing his own scripts, he enjoys going to movies and plays, watching sitcoms, and playing basketball, baseball, and ice hockey. Aidan plans to study filmmaking and screenwriting in college.

CHARLIE GREEN is from Los Angeles, CA. As a self-proclaimed Keatsian Naturalist he seeks escape from LA's urban chaos, so he hopes to have honed his skills as a playwright in the future to move to the Midwest and write plays on a grant. Charlie is inspired by Chekhov, Faulkner, Wallace Stevens, and Howard Barker, and enjoys the avant-garde films of Stan Brakhage and the down-home blues of Charlie Patton. He will be attending Bard College in the fall, where he plans to study Philosophy and Literature.

HAYDIL HENRIQUEZ is from the Bronx, NY. She sees herself working in business or journalism in the future but hopes to publish a book of poetry. Her writing is inspired by the world's injustices and the people around her, specifically her family. Haydil enjoys playing sports and acting, and is indebted to her creative writing teacher, Aracelis Girmay, for helping her discover her own talent.

KEVIN HONG lives in Needham, MA. His writing is mostly influenced by Haruki Murakami and John Cheever, and when he's not crafting a story he can be found playing the piano (which he's done since the age of four), ping-pong, or basketball.

JASMINE HU was born in Beijing, moved to the U.S. at the age of three, and now lives in San Jose, CA. Her hobbies include birdwatching, reading, fretting about current events, cooking, and the corresponding act of eating.

WYNNE HUNGERFORD is from Greenville, SC. She likes antique ice, tumbleweeds, jazz, whitewater kayaking, playing the guitar, and the smell of fishing lures. Another one of her hobbies is not-not writing. In the future she sees herself working on a story or screenplay and spending a lot of time with her eyes closed. She plans to study film and creative writing in college.

MACKENZIE LEE JACOBY is from Provo, UT, "between the Mormons and the mountains." Three men have had a significant impact on her writing: Oscar Wilde, Bruce Springsteen, and Stephen Hawking. When Mackenzie isn't writing she likes to jump into water from ever-higher altitudes, play her accordion, and douse her food in honey.

SHARON JAN attributes her interest in other cultures to the fact that she was born and raised in Southern California, and enjoys drawing and photography as well as writing. She hopes to further inform her multi-cultural sensibilities by attending college outside the United States.

SEAN KAELLNER is from Indianapolis, IN. Among his primary interests are theater, music, art, and traveling. He is inspired by the people around him: his girlfriend Eva, creative writing teacher Lou Debruicker, and his family. He will be attending Indiana University at Bloomington next year, where he will major in Near Eastern Language and Culture.

ERIC KOFMAN lives in Cary, NC. When he's not writing he enjoys playing classical guitar, drawing, painting, golfing, playing tennis, and swimming. He spent the first half of his life in Chile, and his work addresses his memories of growing up abroad. Writers that influence him include Francisco Coloane, Mario Vargas Llosa, and Gabriel García Márquez.

RACHEL KOLB has lived her entire life in the Southwest, in Albuquerque, NM. In high school she completed, edited, and submitted a full-length novel for publication. Outside of literature, her greatest passion is horses—her family owns three—and Rachel's mare, Scarlett O'Hara, has won several state and zone championships. She (Rachel, not Scarlett) will attend Stanford University this fall and plans to major in English.

GABE LEWIN lives in Hopewell, NJ, the quintessential small American town. He is an avid hiker, a cellist, and has a deep, abiding interest in politics. He plans to study Arabic and Hebrew in college.

MATTHEW LLARENA is from Miami Beach, FL. He will be attending Marlboro College in 2008, where he plans to continue studying literature and writing as well as subjects that inspire his writing, like philosophy and botany.

BECKY MCCARTHY attended Greens Farms Academy in Greens Farms, CT. Her short story titled "The Size of a Small Coffin," is about a young woman trying to comfort her older co-worker, as they wait for the older woman's blind date to arrive.

MAXINE MCGREDY is from New York City. In the fourth grade, she told her mother that she first wanted to "write a boring medical tome, then write an exciting medical thriller." She still wants to be a doctor, but plans to write fiction on the side.

GRACE MCNAMEE is from Bethesda, MD. In the future she'd like to work at a publishing house or as a young adult editor, but write novels on the side. Grace is a fan of the work of Dickens, Austen, and Tolstoy, and enjoys swimming and soccer.

PAUL MELCHER lives in Houston, TX. He sees himself as a scientist or comedian in the future. Aside from writing, his primary interests are video games and relaxation. The person who has most significantly impacted his artistic development is his television.

EMMA MORRISON is from Brooklyn, NY. Her most secret desire is to be a breakdancer, Broadway diva, or both. In the future she hopes to write a newspaper column, work as a journalist or editor in fashion, or have amassed enough odd experiences to fill a book written in the style of her hero, David Sedaris. In the fall Emma will be attending the University of Chicago, where she plans to major in English with a focus on creative writing and minor in Psychology.

STEVEN NIEDBALA is from Waynesburg, PA, where he can be found playing the trombone, watching films, and reading dime horror pulps. He cites Ray Bradbury and Francis Ford Coppola as influences in his own work. Steven plans to study a combination of film criticism, philosophy, and English in college.

CLEO O'BRIEN-UDRY is from New Haven, CT. While in labor at a Chicago hospital, her mother watched the *Godfather* trilogy and Cleo attributes the presence of mafia blood in her genetic makeup to this. She likes flash storms, pesto pasta, climbing trees, bass guitars, rain on corrugated iron roofs, late-night movies, flashlight stories, sidewalk poetry, waking up to coffee, the *New York Times*, and NPR, and knowing that, in the end, it's all gonna be okay.

VIRGINIA LEE PFAEHLER was born and raised in Charleston, SC. She began writing in the sixth grade under the tutelage of Rene Bufo Miles. Though prose is a passion, poetry has become her calling. Most of this poetry deals with her tumultuous family, the beautiful Charleston scenery, and the connections she makes between her emotions and her environment. She is a freshman at Warren-Wilson College and hopes to become a Creative Writing teacher.

ALICE RHEE lives in Closter, NJ, and sees a number of possibilities for her future: zooming across Paris on a Vespa, leaning across a balcony in Barcelona, and riding a train across the English countryside. She enjoys glasses of milk with breakfast, seeing the world through her Nikon camera, twisting wildflowers into bracelets, and looking up at the stars. Alice will attend Oberlin College in the fall and plans to major in creative writing.

DANIEL ROSS is from New York City and enjoys casual boating. He tends to write as frequently as possible, due to the fact that he begins foaming at the mouth if he can't get his ideas on paper. Daniel is considering bringing a pet rock into his life.

XINHE SHEN, a raging read-a-holic, lives in San Ramon, CA. In ten years she sees herself in the same place she usually is: lying in bed with her laptop balanced on her legs, trying to come up with something decent to say. Her writing is influenced by an array of old stories from her parents and summer experiences in both urban and rural China, but the aspect of Chinese culture she tends to linger on the most in her writing is the food. She hopes to attend Columbia University for college.

YUMI SHIROMA is from Ardsley, NY. In the microscopic sliver of time she spends not-reading and not-writing, she enjoys drawing and playing the piano. She sees herself as a television producer, screenwriter, or novelist in the future, and wants to thank her parents for helping her self-publish her first novel in the fourth grade—the one with the talking hamsters.

VIVIAN TRUONG lives in Brooklyn, NY. When she isn't writing she can be found fencing and she credits the first flush of her artistic development to her fifth grade teacher, Mrs. Figatner, who assigned her to keep a journal and write in it each day. Vivian will attend Brown University in the fall and plans to major in Literary Arts.

ERIKA TURNER lives in Las Vegas, NV. She will be a 12th grader at Liberty High School in Henderson, NV. Her editorial piece titled "An Inconvenient Truth: No One Cares" is a passionate political call to arms for the younger generation.

MARK WARREN is from New York, NY. His hobbies include playing guitar, listening to music, doing crosswords, basketball, watching sports, and photography. He enjoys the realism of Tim O'Brien and the surrealism of Don DeLillo, and plans to find a job that involves a broad range of topics: writing, history, art, sports, journalism, foreign languages, and humor.

AMELIA WOLF is from Portland, OR. When she's not writing she can be found hiking, skiing, watching *Buffy the Vampire Slayer*, eating out with friends, and surfing wikipedia and reading each article in every language. In the future she sees herself eating Kosher Chinese take-out straight out of the carton, chopstick-sword-fighting with her roommate, and working with a non-profit focusing on girls' education.

NATIONAL WRITING JURORS

AMERICAN VOICES
Phil O'Donoghue
Robert Glass
Kate Rushin

DRAMATIC SCRIPT
Jesse Cameron Alick
Kate E. Ryan
Lori Singer

GENERAL WRITING PORTFOLIO
Jimmy Santiago Baca
Brighde Mullins
Andrea Davis Pinkney
Patricia Smith

HUMOR
Brian Donovan
Ed Herro
David LaRochelle

JOURNALISM
Richard Schlesinger
Charlie Savage
Beagan Wilcox

NONFICTION WRITING PORTFOLIO
Olivia Barker
Brett Blackledge
Art Brisbane

PERSONAL ESSAY/MEMOIR
Pamela Page
Elliott Rebhun
Nancy Youman

POETRY
Carolyn Forche
Alice Quinn
C. K. Williams

SCIENCE FICTION/FANTASY
Danielle Bennett
Holly Black
Elizabeth E. Wein

SHORT STORY
Stephanie Cabot
Aimee Friedman
Lisa Grunwald

SHORT SHORT STORY
Benjamin Cavell
Chuck Palahniuk
Meg Wolitzer

> Want to know more about the national jurors? Go to www.artandwriting.org to read juror biographies.

REGIONAL AFFILIATES

REGIONAL AFFILIATE NETWORK OF THE ALLIANCE FOR YOUNG
ARTISTS & WRITERS
The Alliance partners with Regional Affiliates nationwide that coor-
dinate The Scholastic Art & Writing Awards at the local level. Public
school systems, state education agencies, teacher organizations, art
museums, arts councils, libraries, private foundations, businesses, and
nonprofit organizations in the Network share a deep commitment to
recognizing the creative achievement of young artists and writers in
their areas. The Alliance is grateful to the following organizations and
donors for their efforts to further the Alliance mission of motivating,
validating and encouraging young artists and writers in their communities.

WRITING REGION-AT-LARGE
To provide opportunities for students in areas of the country without
Regional Affiliates, the Alliance for Young Artists & Writers admin-
isters the Region-at-Large Scholastic Writing Awards. Students in
Region-at-Large submit work for preliminary level judging, and
esteemed jurors from across the country evaluate the students' works.
The most outstanding works receive Gold Keys and are forwarded to
the national level of judging.

REGIONAL AFFILIATE ORGANIZATIONS & SPONSORS
The Alliance would like to thank the Regional Affiliates listed on the
following pages and their donors for coordinating The Scholastic Art
& Writing Awards in their areas.

CALIFORNIA
San Francisco Unified School District
San Francisco Writing Region

DELAWARE
The Arts Center/Gallery at Delaware
Delaware Writing Region
Delaware State University
Additional Sponsors: Wesley College, The Art Educators of Delaware, The Denver Post, Inc., Colonial Rotary, and through the generosity of private donors

FLORIDA
Miami-Dade County Public Schools
Miami-Dade Writing Region

Pinellas County Public Schools
Pinellas County Writing Region
Additional Sponsors: General Dynamics, Raymond James Financial, and Festival of States

INDIANA & OHIO
Fort Wayne Museum of Art
Northeast Indiana and Northwest Ohio Writing Region
Additional Sponsors: JP Morgan Chase and News-Sentinel

KENTUCKY
Northern Kentucky University, College of Arts and Sciences, Department of Literature and Language
Northern Kentucky Writing Region

Additional Sponsors: Northern Kentucky University College of Arts & Sciences, Northern Kentucky University Department of Literature & Language, Thomas More College, and Staples, Inc.

_____

MISSISSIPPI
Eudora Welty Foundation
Mississippi Writing Region

_____

MISSOURI
Prairie Lands Writing Project at Missouri Western State University
Missouri Writing Region
Additional Sponsors: Missouri Writing Projects Network and Missouri Association of Teachers of English

_____

NEVADA
Nevada Foundation for the Arts
Southern Nevada Writing Region

_____

NEW YORK
Alliance for Young Artists & Writers, Inc.
New York City Writing Region
Additional Sponsors: Scholastic, Inc., The Maurice R. Robinson Fund, The Jack Kent Cooke Foundation, Command Web Offset, CDW-G, The New York Times Company, Dell, Quebecorworld, Bloomberg LP, Ovation TV, The Richard and Mica Hadar Foundation, and Three Bridge Trust

_____

NORTH CAROLINA
Charlotte-Mecklenburg Schools, Arts Education Department
Mid-Carolina Writing Region

Public Library of Charlotte & Mecklenburg County
Mid-Carolina Writing Region

___

PENNSYLVANIA
Lancaster County Public Library
Lancaster County Writing Region

The Patriot-News Co.
Central Pennsylvania Writing Region

Waynesburg College
Southwestern Pennsylvania Writing Region
Additional Sponsors: CONSOL Energy, Pennsylvania Rural Arts
    Alliance, Community Foundation of Greene County, Observer
    Reporter, and Friends of the Arts in Greene, Fayette, and Washington
    Counties

___

TEXAS
Harris County Department of Education
Harris County Writing Region
Additional Sponsors: Women in the Visual and Literary Arts, Indo-
    American Charity Foundation, University of St. Thomas, School of
    Education, Houston Chronicle, and Barnes & Noble Booksellers

___

VERMONT
Great River Arts Institute
Vermont Writing Region

___

VIRGINIA
The Visual Arts Center of Richmond
Metro Area Richmond Writing Region

PARTNERSHIP OPPORTUNITIES

SUPPORT THE CREATIVE ACHIEVEMENT OF YOUNG WRITERS: JOIN THE REGIONAL AFFILIATE NETWORK OF THE ALLIANCE FOR YOUNG ARTISTS & WRITERS

By joining the Regional Affiliate Network, your organization can:

- Increase opportunities for teenagers to receive regional and national recognition for their creative talent, publish their works, and receive scholarships;
- Create connections among students, teachers, schools, and language arts organizations in your community;
- Enhance your organization's visibility as part of a long-standing national network that supports young writers.

For more information on becoming a Regional Affiliate of the Alliance for Young Artists & Writers, please contact Kat Hendrix at khendrix@scholastic.com or 212.343.7774.

ALLIANCE SCHOLARSHIP PROVIDER NETWORK

The Alliance would also like to thank the colleges and universities that provide scholarships to national Scholastic Art & Writing Awards recipients in writing categories. These include: Bard College, College of Mt. St. Joseph, Brewton Parker College, University of Maine Farmington, Kansas State University, Kenyon College, and Bennington College. To learn more about the Alliance Scholarship Provider Network, please contact Kat Hendrix at khendrix@scholastic.com or 212.343.7774.

ABOUT THE ALLIANCE FOR YOUNG ARTISTS & WRITERS

The Alliance for Young Artists & Writers continues to bring outstanding visual arts and writing created by teenagers to a national audience by showcasing their remarkable work and encouraging their creative journey and career development. The Alliance, a nonprofit organization, was formed in 1994 to support aspiring young artists and writers through The Scholastic Art & Writing Awards program. The Alliance seeks to identify emerging artists for college scholarship consideration, and invests in the critical role of creative development for students by offering six years of eligibility beginning in seventh grade. The Alliance also collaborates with colleges across the country to leverage an additional $3.25 million in financial aid for award recipients who demonstrate exceptional promise.

Special projects of the Alliance include:

THE NATIONAL ART EXHIBITION OF THE SCHOLASTIC ART & WRITING AWARDS, an exhibition held in New York City each June of national award-winning work by America's most talented teenagers;

THE SCHOLASTIC ART & WRITING AWARDS NATIONAL CATALOG, an annual publication that showcases nationally recognized work;

ONLINE EXHIBITIONS AND ANTHOLOGIES, a selection of artwork and writing published online at www.artandwriting.org;

THE BEST TEEN WRITING, an annual anthology of teen writing from The Scholastic Writing Awards;

SPARK: YOUNG VOICES AND VISIONS, a publication showcasing the work of emerging young artists and writers from 7th and 8th grades from across the country;

PUSH ANTHOLOGIES: THE BEST YOUNG WRITERS AND ARTISTS IN AMERICA (published by Scholastic Inc.)
You Are Here, This Is Now
Where We Are, What We See
We Are Quiet, We Are Loud

Visit www.artandwriting.org for more information about the Alliance, including participation information for The Scholastic Art & Writing Awards of 2009 and to view the Virtual Gallery of nationally recognized work.

ALLIANCE BOARD AND STAFF

OPPORTUNITIES FOR CREATIVE TEENS

The Scholastic Art & Writing Awards offer early recognition of creative teenagers and scholarship opportunities for graduating high school seniors. Supported by their visual arts and writing teachers and other community mentors, participants create and submit their best works in any of the following categories:

VISUAL ARTS

Art Portfolio, Animation, Ceramics & Glass, Computer Art, Design, Drawing, Graphic Story, Mixed Media, Painting, Photography, Photography Portfolio, Printmaking, Sculpture, Video & Film

WRITING

Dramatic Script, General Writing Portfolio, Humor, Journalism, Nonfiction Portfolio, Novel, Personal Essay/Memoir, Poetry, Science Fiction/Fantasy, Short Story, Short Short Story

Each October, program materials are made available to students in grades 7–12.

High school seniors who submit portfolios compete for more than $3.25 million in tuition scholarships at colleges across the nation. Twelve $10,000 scholarships are presented to Portfolio Gold Award recipients in art, photography, and writing.

Visit our Web site at www.artandwriting.org to learn more about The Awards, for deadlines and entry information, and to view galleries of previous national award-winning art and writing.

HOW TO DONATE

SUPPORT THE ALLIANCE FOR YOUNG ARTISTS & WRITERS
Please support our work developing opportunities for creative young people. Donations to the Alliance help underwrite national and NYC-based programs that create Recognition, Exhibition, Publication, and Scholarship opportunities for our nation's most creative teens.

Please help us continue our work by making a donation today:

By Check
Mail to:
Alliance for Young Artists & Writers, Inc.
557 Broadway
New York, NY 10012

By Credit Card
Visit www.artandwriting.org, click DonateNow to make a secure donation.

Donations to the Alliance for Young Artists & Writers are tax-deductible to the fullest extent of the law.

For more information, contact Venas Matthews, Senior Manager, External Relations, by phone at 212.343.7717 or by email at vmatthews@scholastic.com.